THE IT PARADOX

REIMAGINE, TRANSFORM, THRIVE, YOUR ROADMAP TO THE FUTURE OF BANKING STARTS HERE.

MASTERING CHANGE IN BANKING'S DIGITAL JOURNEY

VIJAY VASUDEVAN

ISBN
Hardcase 979-8-89724-908-4
Paperback 979-8-89699-915-7

CONTENTS

Guiding Principle from Mahabharata for this book.

Shloka from Udyoga Parva (Chapter 33, Verse 38):

"Vyavasāyātmikā buddhir ekeha kuru-nandana, Bahu-śhākhā hyanantāśh cha buddhayo 'vyavasāyinām."

Translation:

"In this world, O son of the Kuru dynasty, resolute intelligence is one-pointed and focused. But the thoughts of the irresolute are many-branched and endless."

This shloka emphasizes the importance of focus, determination, and clarity in navigating complex paths, such as digital transformation. It highlights the need for organizations to have a clear, singular vision, rather than being distracted by countless possibilities. Leaders and teams embarking on transformation journeys must prioritize resilience and purpose to succeed.

FOREWORD

From Mr. Arun Diaz

During my tenure as a Director at Suryoday SFB, I had the opportunity of working with Vijay Vasudevan, a self-driven and innovative professional.

Although our association was brief, I was impressed with Vijay's ability to leverage technology to achieve strategic business goals, by enhancing operational efficiencies or creating customer-centric solutions.

He was also able to build and implement IP-driven solutions in Collections and Legal processes which addressed key business challenges while setting new benchmarks for efficiency and scalability.

His collaborative mindset and leadership skills enabled him to work seamlessly across functions, fostering a culture of innovation and teamwork whilst also driving change in the organization. His ability to inspire and empower those around him has been instrumental in building high-performing teams and achieving remarkable outcomes.

Having witnessed his contributions firsthand. I am confident that his expertise, passion, and visionary approach will continue to make a profound impact in every role he undertakes.

Arun Diaz

Independent Director, *Suryoday Small Finance Bank, Arohan Financial Services Limited, Collateral Medical Private Limited, and several other esteemed organizations.*

From Mr. Balaji Vasudevan

I am truly delighted to write the foreword for The IT Paradox: Mastering Change in Banking's Digital Journey, a remarkable work by Vijay Vasudevan. With nearly 25 years of experience as a techno-functional specialist in the banking industry, Vijay brings a wealth of expertise to this book. His passion for learning and constant pursuit of new skills has been evident since his early years.

A true go-getter, he never rests until a task is completed to the highest standard. Vijay consistently pushes himself beyond his limits to achieve excellence in everything he undertakes. He is not someone who simply embraces theory; rather, he believes in testing concepts through practical application.

ABOUT THIS BOOK

In a world where change is relentless and technology is advancing at an unprecedented rate, "digital transformation" has evolved from a buzzword to a critical necessity. However, as this book will demonstrate, digital transformation is not simply about implementing the latest technologies or adopting cutting-edge tools. At its heart, it revolves around the people who drive it, the vision that inspires it, and the persistence needed to sustain it.

Digital transformation is fundamentally a shift in mindset—a recognition that technology serves as an enabler, not the end goal. It's about fostering a culture where innovation thrives, where organizations can adapt to disruption, and where individuals are empowered to transform both themselves and their environments.

As you journey through the pages of this book, you will discover that true transformation goes beyond revolutionizing industries; it is equally about embracing change on a personal level. Whether you are a leader guiding your organization through the complexities of digital disruption or an individual striving to navigate a rapidly evolving digital landscape, the insights within will help you build a resilient, forward-thinking future.

This book offers more than just theoretical ideas; it presents practical wisdom, real-world examples, and actionable strategies to help you thrive in the age of digital transformation. It's a call to those who are ready to embrace change, lead with vision, and persist even when the path forward seems unclear.

Digital transformation is not a singular event, but a continuous journey. This book will act as your guide to not only making this journey possible but also rewarding.

I wish Vijay Vasudevan the very best in his endeavour to publish this book. I am confident that he has many more valuable topics to share in the upcoming series.

Regards

Balaji Vasudevan Iyengar

Chief Executive Officer & Managing Director,

Sysarc Infomatix, a CSI Co.

PREFACE

The banking industry is transforming, but the journey isn't easy. While digital innovation holds the potential to revolutionize how banks operate and serve their customers, it often meets resistance from legacy systems, traditional processes, and most importantly people. This paradox of technology, the tension between its promise and the hurdles in its adoption has been the central theme of my career.

I began my professional journey with a degree in commerce from the interior part of Tamil Nadu called Trichy, stepped into the world of banking with curiosity and enthusiasm in the economic capital of India, Mumbai in 2001. Over the last 25 years, I've had the privilege of working with some of the most respected names in the industry, including CITI, HDFC, HSBC, Sundaram, Dhan Laxmi Bank, Tata Group, Suryoday & Equitas Bank etc. These experiences exposed me to the inner workings of banking, from sales and collections to credit and risk, helping me understand what drives this intricate ecosystem.

As my career progressed, I've realized that technology was no longer just a tool but a necessity for survival and growth in the financial sector. This realization led me to transition into roles focused on business transformation and technology leadership. To equip myself for these challenges, I pursued the CIO Certification from Carnegie Mellon University,

Pittsburgh, USA a turning point that gave me the confidence and skills to lead large-scale digital transformations.

Over the years, I've worked on a range of transformative initiatives in banks and NBFCs. My deep grounding in sales, collections, and strategy helped me bridge the gap between business needs and technological solutions, ensuring that technology didn't just automate processes but solved real problems. I've seen firsthand how people respond to the change, some embrace it, while others resist it fiercely. Understanding and addressing these human aspects is as critical to transformation as implementing the right technology.

This book, ***"The IT Paradox: Mastering Change in Banking's Digital Journey"***, is a reflection of my journey. It explores what it takes to make a bank truly digital, not just in systems, but in culture and mindset. I share stories of successes and setbacks, the lessons I've learned, and how I've seen effective partnerships between business and IT leaders in achieving incredible results.

At its heart, this book is for those who believe in the power of transformation. Whether you're a leader navigating the challenges of change, or a professional looking to make sense of digital disruption, or someone curious about what it takes to lead a bank into the future, I hope this book resonates with you.

Digital transformation is not just about technology, it's about people, vision, and persistence. Together, let's explore how we can embrace the IT paradox and build a banking future that's innovative, efficient, and deeply human.

This book reflects my journey and learnings from 25 years in the banking industry. To ensure a smooth and polished reading experience, I have relied on tools like Copilot for creating images and ChatGPT for refining the language and enhancing sentence structure. While these tools have helped in presentation, the ideas, strategies, and experiences are entirely my own.

Vijay Vasudevan

"Success in a digital age is not just about dopting new technology—it's about building a culture that is prepared to embrace change."

– Satya Nadella

01

WHY IT IS A PARADOX?

When we talk about Information Technology (IT) in today's world, it often feels like both a blessing and a burden, an incredible tool that has the power to transform everything, but one that can be hard to embrace fully. In industries like banking, where tradition runs deep and systems have been in place for years, this paradox is even more apparent. IT promises a brighter, faster, and more efficient future, but it also brings with it challenges, uncertainties, and resistance.

Here's why IT feels like a paradox:

Innovation vs. Tradition: IT is the gateway to innovation, new technologies, new ways of working, and new ways of serving customers. But in industries like banking, where practices and systems have been built over decades, change can feel like a threat. The comfort of the familiar can often outweigh the excitement of the new. While digital transformation promises faster, smoother processes, breaking away from traditional methods can feel like stepping into uncharted territory. It's like having the map to a new world but still being attached to the old ways.

Efficiency vs. Complexity: Technology is supposed to simplify things, make work more efficient, and free up time for more strategic thinking. But the reality is often the opposite. Implementing new IT systems can feel like adding layers of complexity, more software to learn, more processes to manage, more data to sift through. The promise of greater efficiency sometimes creates more headaches as teams are forced to learn and adapt to the new tools and systems. It's a bit like trying to clean your house but realizing you've just made more mess along the way.

Automation vs. Human Touch: We're constantly told that automation will make us faster and more accurate. But in industries like banking, where relationships and trust are the cornerstone of success, replacing human interactions with automated systems can feel cold and impersonal. It's a paradox: we want faster, more efficient service, but we don't want to lose the personal touch. Customers want the convenience of digital banking, but they also want to feel like someone is listening when they have a problem. The key is to balance both-technology that enhances the human connection, not replaces it.

Security vs. Accessibility: One of the great promises of IT is that it gives us easy access to information and services from anywhere. But with that accessibility comes a huge responsibility: keeping all that data safe. The more accessible something is, the more exposed it becomes to potential threats. It's a balancing act. We want to make it easy for our employees and customers to access what they need, but at the same time, we need to ensure their data remains secure. It's a constant dance between making things convenient and making sure they're safe.

Speed vs. Reliability: In the digital world, we all expect things to happen instantly. We want everything now, quick answers, fast transactions, instant gratification. But speed often comes at the cost of reliability. New technologies might promise lightning-fast results, but they aren't always as dependable as the older, slower systems. We're caught between the desire to be fast and the need to be steady, and that's where the paradox lies. Quick can be great, but not at the expense of trustworthiness.

Adaptability vs. Resistance to Change: Every digital transformation requires change and change is hard. People are often set in their ways, especially when the systems they've worked with for years have served them well. The introduction of new technology might be met with excitement from some, but it's usually met with resistance from others. It's one of the toughest challenges in digital transformation: getting people to not just adopt new tools but embrace a new mindset. It's like upgrading your phone to the latest model but not being ready to let go of the old one that still works just fine.

At the heart of this paradox is a simple truth: while IT offers incredible potential to make things faster, smarter, and more efficient, it's never as simple as just flipping a switch. It requires understanding, patience, and a willingness to adapt. And perhaps most importantly, it requires people leaders who can guide teams through the inevitable growing pains, and individuals who are ready to embrace the future while respecting the past. The paradox is only resolved when we find the right balance between the promises of technology and the realities of human behaviour.

02

WHERE LEGACY MEETS OPPORTUNITY

The banking industry stands at a fascinating crossroads—a place where tradition meets transformation, and where opportunities are as vast as the challenges they bring. Over the years, I've had the privilege of witnessing and driving the digital transformation journeys of several banks and financial institutions. These experiences have shown me that digital transformation isn't just about technology; it's about people, culture, and the way organizations adapt—or resist—change.

This book, "The IT Paradox: Mastering Change in Banking's Digital Journey," is a reflection of that journey. It's about the tug-of-war between progress and hesitation, about the remarkable successes and frustrating setbacks that arise when we try to bridge the gap between what's possible and what's comfortable. It's also about the critical role that collaboration between business and IT plays in achieving lasting transformation, especially in an industry that often views technology as a cost centre rather than a driver of growth.

Through this book, I aim to address the challenges that often go unspoken—the resistance from teams down the line, the hesitation to adopt changes that feel imposed by leadership, and the focus on individual credit over collective success. I'll also share stories, insights, and actionable guidance for both business and IT leaders, helping them align their efforts toward a common goal: building a truly digital bank that puts the organization's vision first.

Above all, this book is a call to action for leaders to see digital transformation not as a technology project but as a cultural shift—one that requires every individual in the organization to play their part. Together, we can navigate the paradox of IT and lead the banking industry into its digital future.

WHAT IS DIGITAL TRANSFORMATION?

Digital transformation is about rethinking how businesses operate and how they connect with people, powered by technology. In banking, it's not just swapping ledgers for computers or branches for apps, it's about making banking smarter, faster, and more accessible for everyone. It's the reason you can transfer money in seconds, apply for a loan from your living room, or get real-time updates on your investments with a simple tap.

But digital transformation goes beyond convenience. It's about creating experiences that feel personal and intuitive, where technology works seamlessly in the background to make things easier. For banks, it's also about staying relevant in a world where customer expectations are sky-high and competition isn't just other banks, it's also fintech's, wallets, and global tech giants.

At its heart, digital transformation is a mindset. It's a commitment to embracing change, putting customers first, and building a future where banking is not just a service but a seamless part of everyday life. It's the journey of moving from traditional ways to innovative solutions, ensuring no one is left behind in the process.

3.1. Defining Digital Transformation in Banking

Banking has come a long way from its humble beginnings of manually updated ledgers and handwritten passbooks. In those days, banking was a slow, meticulous process. Customers would visit their local branches, wait in queues, and rely on the bank staff to record their debits and credits. Every transaction required physical presence, personal interaction, and trust built on face-to-face communication.

Fast forward to today, and banking looks completely different. We're in an era where technology has redefined not just how banking is done but also how it's perceived. Digital banking is no longer a luxury but an expectation. For many of us, me included, visiting a bank branch has become an outdated concept. Personally, I can't even recall the last time I went to a branch to deposit or withdraw money. My relationship with my bank is now entirely digital, from fund transfers to bill payments and investments, all done at the tap of a screen.

The Indian Government's Digital Push

This shift isn't happening in isolation; it's part of a broader movement led by the Indian government's **Digital India** initiative. The aim is clear: to transform India into a digitally empowered society and knowledge economy. This vision includes ensuring that government services are made available to citizens electronically, reducing paperwork, and increasing accessibility.

In the banking sector, this strategy has accelerated initiatives like:

- **UPI (Unified Payments Interface):** Revolutionizing real-time payments and making financial transactions seamless for millions.

- **Digital Lending Platforms:** Empowering small businesses and individuals to access credit through streamlined digital processes.

- **Account Aggregators:** Simplifying access to financial data for individuals and institutions alike.

- **e-RUPI:** Promoting cashless and contactless payment systems.

These initiatives are creating a ripple effect, pushing banks to adopt digital-first strategies to align with national goals and customer expectations.

What Does Digital Transformation in Banking Really Mean?

Digital transformation in banking goes beyond adopting new technologies; it's about rethinking processes, customer interactions, and the overall role of a bank in a digital economy. It involves:

1. **Enhancing Customer Experience:** Offering seamless, personalized, and convenient banking services through mobile apps, chatbots, and AI-driven solutions.

2. **Streamlining Operations:** Using automation, cloud computing, and data analytics to reduce costs and improve efficiency.

3. **Ensuring Security:** Adopting cutting-edge cybersecurity measures to protect customers' data and transactions.

4. **Building Agility:** Developing systems and processes that can adapt quickly to changing customer needs and regulatory landscapes.

The Journey to 100% Digital Banking

Indian banks are actively working towards becoming fully digital entities. From paperless onboarding and digital KYC processes to AI-driven customer service, the goal is to create a banking experience that requires minimal physical interaction while maximizing convenience and security. However, this journey isn't without its challenges:

- Convincing customers in rural and semi-urban areas to adopt digital banking.

- Ensuring data privacy and compliance with regulatory frameworks.

- Aligning organizational culture to embrace innovation and technology.

In this chapter, we explore the transition from traditional to digital banking, the driving forces behind it, and the strategies required to navigate this shift. Digital transformation is not just a technological upgrade; it's a redefinition of banking itself a journey from ledgers to algorithms, from branches to bytes.

3.2. The Opportunities Digital Transformation Brings to Banks

In the world of banking, customers are like fish in the ocean—elusive and ever-moving. To serve them effectively, banks must act swiftly, addressing their needs almost instantly. Delays can lead to lost opportunities and, worse, losing the customer to a competitor. Digital transformation presents banks and financial institutions with unprecedented opportunities to reach, engage, and serve customers, especially in untapped and underserved markets.

Reaching the Untapped Market in India

India is home to a vast and diverse population, but a significant portion of it remains unbanked or underserved by formal financial institutions. The **untapped opportunities** for banks can be categorized into:

1. **Geographic Reach:** Despite India's extensive banking network, it's nearly impossible for a bank to have physical branches in every one of the country's 250,000+ villages. This creates a significant gap in financial inclusion, especially in rural and semi-urban areas. Digital banking eliminates this barrier, enabling institutions to provide services in the most remote corners of the nation.

2. **Customer Segments:** A large percentage of the Indian population's financial needs are still met by **unorganized financial players**, moneylenders, chit funds, or informal credit networks. Studies suggest that nearly **30% of India's adult population** still relies on these unregulated sources for their financial needs. Digital transformation can help banks tap into these segments, offering them formal financial services like loans, savings accounts, and insurance with better security and transparency.

3. **Jan Dhan Yojana and Financial Inclusion:** The **Pradhan Mantri Jan Dhan Yojana (PMJDY)** has successfully brought millions of underprivileged individuals into the banking system. Today, almost every villager and farmer have a bank account. However, most of these accounts are used primarily to receive government benefits.

Imagine the potential if banks actively engage with these account holders to:

- Offer small-ticket loans to farmers and rural entrepreneurs.

- Build their creditworthiness through micro-lending initiatives.

- Provide them with financial literacy and tools to manage their funds more effectively.

This isn't just about capturing new markets; it's about transforming lives and contributing to **nation-building**.

Empowering rural customers through financial services can uplift entire communities, leading to sustained economic growth.

The Immediate Advantage of Digital Banking

Digital transformation equips banks to:

- **Serve Instantly:** With real-time data and analytics, banks can address customer needs immediately, whether it's approving a loan, resolving a query, or providing tailored financial products.

- **Reach New Customers:** Mobile banking apps, digital wallets, and AI-driven chatbots allow banks to connect with customers who may never visit a branch.

- **Reduce Costs:** Operating digitally eliminates the overheads of physical infrastructure, making it feasible to serve low-income and remote customers profitably.

A Nation-Building Strategy

Banks and financial institutions have a critical role in India's development story. By leveraging digital transformation:

- They can provide **microloans** to farmers, small businesses, and underserved individuals.

- They can foster **financial literacy**, encouraging customers to save, invest, and manage their finances effectively.

- They can contribute to **economic inclusion**, ensuring that the benefits of India's growth reach every corner of the country.

Digital transformation is not just a business strategy, it's a way for banks to fulfil their larger responsibility as agents of progress. It enables them to bring financial services to the underserved and unlock their potential, creating opportunities that benefit both the institution and the nation.

In this chapter, we explore the immense possibilities that digital transformation offers to banks, the untapped market potential in India, and the strategic role of digital banking in empowering customers and communities alike. The opportunities are vast, but realizing them requires vision, commitment, and innovation.

3.3. How IT aligns with CX and Competitive Dynamics

In today's fast-paced world, customer's expectations are evolving faster than ever before, reshaping industries including banking. The convenience of technology has redefined how people interact with services, demanding speed, simplicity, and personalization. For banks and financial institutions, aligning with these expectations isn't just an option, it's essential for survival. At the same time, the competitive landscape has expanded, with fintech players, digital wallets, and tech giants stepping in to fill the gaps traditional banks once owned.

This section explores how digital transformation addresses these dual pressures: meeting ever-rising customer demands while staying competitive in a rapidly changing market. From offering seamless experiences to building trust through transparency, we'll dive into the keyways banks can stay ahead by truly understanding and serving their customers. After all, it's not just about adopting technology; it's about reimagining banking in a way that resonates with people and creates lasting loyalty.

1. Customers Demand Convenience, Not Excuses

Let's be honest, no one has time to stand in long lines or fill out endless forms anymore. Today's customers want banking to be as simple as ordering food or booking a cab. They expect services to be quick, easy, and available anytime, anywhere. Digital transformation helps banks meet this need, offering mobile apps, instant approvals, and seamless experiences. If a bank can't provide this level of convenience, customers will simply move on to one that can.

2. People Want to Be Treated as Individuals

Everyone wants to feel valued, and banking is no different. Customers don't just want generic services; they want personalized solutions tailored to their needs and goals. Through digital tools like AI and data analytics, banks can now understand customers better than ever before. They can offer a savings plan for a young professional, a home loan for a growing family, or investment advice for retirees. When people feel understood, they stay loyal.

3. Speed and Simplicity Win Every Time

Let's face it, no one enjoys complicated processes. Whether it's opening an account or applying for a loan, customers expect things to happen fast and without unnecessary hassles. Digital transformation cuts through the red tape, automating processes so customers get what they need in minutes, not days. In a world where speed is everything, being fast is a bank's biggest competitive advantage.

4. Trust Through Transparency

Money is personal, and trust is non-negotiable. Customers expect clarity—whether it's about fees, terms, or the status of their transactions. With digital platforms, banks can give customers real-time updates and detailed insights into their accounts. When customers know exactly what's happening with their money, they trust the institution—and trust is what keeps them coming back.

5. Competing With the New Kids on the Block

It's not just other banks competing for customers anymore. Fintech startups, digital wallets, and even tech giants are offering innovative financial solutions that are fast, user-friendly, and tech driven. If traditional banks don't step up, they risk becoming obsolete. Digital transformation isn't just about staying relevant—it's about staying in the game.

6. Living Up to Global Expectations

Today's customers don't just compare banks to each other, they compare them to global experiences. Whether it's a slick app or lightning-fast service, they expect the same quality from their bank that they get from any global tech company. Digital transformation helps banks deliver world-class services while staying rooted in local realities.

7. Loyalty Is Earned, Not Given

Gone are the days when customers stuck with a bank just because their parents did. Today, loyalty is built on how well a bank engages with its customers. Digital tools make it possible to stay connected—sending reminders, offering personalized tips, or resolving issues in real-time. When customers feel cared for and engaged, they're less likely to switch to someone else.

At its core, digital transformation is about more than technology. It's about understanding what customers truly want and delivering it with speed, simplicity, and trust. It's also about recognizing the new competitive reality: the fight isn't just with other banks; it's with anyone who can offer a better, faster, and easier way to manage money. To succeed, banks must not only adapt, but they must also lead the way.

> **"A satisfied customer is the best business strategy of all."**
>
> **– Michael LeBoeuf**

04

THE CULTURAL CHALLENGE: PEOPLE AND RESISTANCE

One of the biggest hurdles in any digital transformation journey isn't technology, it's people. It's human nature to resist change, especially when it feels like it disrupts the familiar process or threatens personal comfort zones. In the world of banking, this resistance often stems from deeply rooted cultures, established processes, and the pursuit of individual or departmental goals over organizational priorities. This is where the "organization first" approach becomes crucial.

4.1. Organization First Approach

Digital transformation, at its core, is about making things better for the organization, for its employees, and for its customers. But often, what should be an exciting journey of improvement becomes a battle against resistance. Why? Because change, even positive change, is uncomfortable.

In many banks and financial institutions, resistance to change is a reality across departments whether it's Sales, Credit, Operations, or Collections. People are used to their routines and comfortable with their current processes, even if those processes are outdated or inefficient. Any new system or transformation disrupts this comfort zone, and for many, that disruption feels more like a burden than an opportunity.

Ironically, even when the proposed changes promise to boost productivity or simplify tasks, hesitation remains. This is partly because people often don't see the immediate benefits for themselves. A common, unspoken question arises: "What's in it for me?" Without clear answers, enthusiasm dwindles.

Another significant barrier is the lack of time invested by key stakeholders. In the fast-paced world of banking, where day-to-day tasks often feel overwhelming, transformation can feel like a distraction rather than a priority. But here's the truth: without quality time and commitment from those involved, no transformation can succeed. Stakeholders need to actively participate, provide insights, and champion the change within their teams.

Adopting an "organization-first" mindset is critical to overcoming these challenges. This means looking beyond individual tasks, departments, or personal gains and focusing on how transformation serves the greater good. It's about understanding that when the organization thrives, everyone benefits.

Change isn't easy, but with clear communication, empathy, and a shared vision, teams can move from resistance to collaboration, paving the way for meaningful and lasting transformation.

4.1.1. Organizational goals must take precedence over individual

One of the biggest roadblocks in any transformation journey is the fear of change—particularly the fear that automation or new processes might diminish an individual's importance in the organization. This fear often leads to resistance, hesitation, and, at times, even deliberate non-cooperation. It's a natural reaction, rooted in a desire to protect one's role and value. But this mindset, while human, can become a significant barrier to progress—not just for the organization but for the individuals themselves.

Let me share a personal experience that illustrates this perfectly. When I was leading a digital transformation initiative, one of my key goals was to identify critical operational processes that were manual, error-prone, and could potentially lead to financial or reputational risks. The idea was to automate these processes using Robotic Process Automation (RPA), delivering faster, more accurate results while freeing up resources for more strategic tasks.

One such process was Bank Reconciliation and the NACH (National Automated Clearing House) process. These were entirely manual and heavily dependent on a single individual who had been handling them for years. This person's expertise in the processes was undeniable, but so was the vulnerability, it was a single point of failure for the organization.

When I approached him to document the process for automation, I encountered immense resistance. He was visibly uncomfortable and even hesitant to share the details. As I probed further, he finally opened up, saying, "If you automate this, I'll lose my importance in the organization." His fear was genuine, he had spent years mastering this process and had built his identity and value around it.

This was a turning point for me as a leader. It was clear that pushing forward without addressing his concerns would only deepen the resistance. So, I sat down with him and had an open, honest conversation. I explained how automation wasn't about taking away his value but amplifying it. By automating repetitive tasks, he could focus on higher-value work, become a mentor for others, and take on new responsibilities. It wasn't about replacing him but about empowering him to contribute in more meaningful ways.

Eventually, he agreed to collaborate, albeit cautiously. We successfully automated the process, and the results were remarkable, faster execution, zero errors, and significant operational efficiency. But what stood out most to me was his reaction after seeing the success. Far from feeling diminished, he was proud. That year, he even won an award for accuracy in Bank Reconciliation, a recognition that highlighted how his role had evolved, and his contributions were invaluable to the organization.

This experience reinforced a crucial lesson: transformation is not just about systems and processes, it's about people. When individuals resist change, it's often because they feel threatened or undervalued. As leaders, it's our responsibility to address these fears, show them the bigger picture, and help them understand how their growth aligns with the organization's success.

An organization-first approach doesn't mean ignoring individual contributions; it means ensuring that all person's efforts contribute to the collective goal. When individuals focus solely on safeguarding their roles, they inadvertently hold the organization back. But when they align their personal growth with organizational objectives, it creates a win-win situation—one where both the individual and the organization can thrive.

Ultimately, the goal of digital transformation is not to replace people but to empower them. By prioritizing organizational goals, we not only drive progress but also create an environment where everyone feels valued and has the opportunity to grow. Change, after all, is only as successful as the people behind it.

IT Strategy inline with Business Strategy

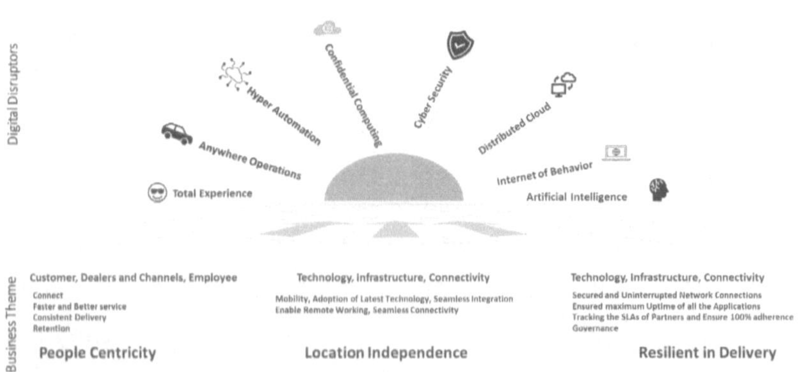

4.1.2. Aligning teams with a shared vision of digital success

Digital transformation in banking is not just a technology upgrade; it's a cultural shift that requires a collective effort from all teams across the organization. No single process in a bank operates in isolation—it's always a collaborative web of cross-functional contributions. This interconnectedness means that the success of any digital initiative depends on every team, from the front office to the back end, moving in unison toward a shared goal.

Collaboration Beyond Silos

One of the greatest challenges in digital transformation is breaking down organizational silos. Each team—be it sales, credit, operations, or collections—often focuses on its immediate responsibilities, which can create blind spots in the larger picture. For example, if the operations team isn't fully aligned with a transformation project initiated by the business team, the entire effort can falter. This disconnect can lead to delays, miscommunication, and ultimately, a lack of adoption. To succeed, teams must shift their perspective from "this is my job" to "this is our mission."

Recognition Fuels Motivation

A recurring issue in many organizations is the perception of unequal recognition. In banking, for instance, the business team often receives accolades for driving revenue, while the operations or credit teams—whose efforts are essential to ensuring smooth execution—go unnoticed. This imbalance can breed resentment and disengagement. Aligning teams with a shared vision of digital success means acknowledging the contributions of all players, not just the stars on the frontlines. Leadership must actively create a culture where every effort, no matter how behind-the-scenes it may seem, is celebrated as part of the bigger picture.

Shared Goals Over Individual KPIs

Most teams operate with their own KPIs, which are often at odds with those of other teams. For instance, while a sales team might prioritize speed in customer onboarding, the credit team might focus on thorough checks to mitigate risk. These conflicting priorities can derail transformation projects. A shared vision requires aligning KPIs with the organization's broader digital goals, ensuring that every team sees how their work contributes to the collective outcome.

The Backbone of Transformation

Let's consider an example: automating a loan approval process in a bank. While the business team may be the face of this transformation, the heavy lifting—system integration, compliance checks, and document verification—falls to operations and IT. If the operations team resists the change, fearing job redundancy or disruption to their routine, the project is doomed before it begins. Success comes when every team understands that their role is indispensable in creating a seamless customer experience, and that transformation is not about replacing people but empowering them.

Empathy and Communication are Key

To align teams, leaders must foster open dialogue and empathy. Transformation often feels threatening to employees who are comfortable with existing processes. Taking the time to explain the "why" behind the change—how it benefits not just the organization but also their individual growth—can make a world of difference. Regular updates, transparent communication, and involving all teams in decision-making create a sense of ownership and reduce resistance.

Success Stories to Inspire Alignment

I've seen firsthand how a shared vision can drive transformation. In one of my previous roles, we introduced a customer self-service portal that required input from sales, IT, and operations. Initially, the operations team resisted, feeling it added to their workload without clear benefits. But as the portal began reducing manual tasks and errors, their enthusiasm grew. The project's success wasn't just in the technology—it was in the collective effort of aligned teams working toward a common goal.

In the end, aligning teams with a shared vision isn't just about processes or systems; it's about people. It's about showing them that their efforts matter, that their fears are heard, and that their contributions are vital to the organization's success. When teams move together with trust, understanding, and recognition, digital transformation becomes not just possible, but inevitable.

> **"No member of a crew is praised for the rugged individuality of his rowing."**
>
> **– Ralph Waldo Emerson**

4.2. Role of Business in Digital Transformation

Digital transformation is not merely a technological initiative, it is a collaborative journey, and at its heart lies the business teams. Whether it is Sales, Credit, Operations, Collections, Legal, Compliance, or Audit, these teams are the primary consumers of the IT applications delivered by the technology department. Their role is pivotal in ensuring the success of any transformation initiative, as they are the ones who understand the processes and challenges intimately, from the frontlines to the back office.

The business teams hold the responsibility of identifying the processes that need digitization. They are the architects of the "what" and "why" of transformation. It is their role to analyse existing workflows, identify bottlenecks, and determine which processes, if automated or digitized, can lead to better efficiency, accuracy, and customer satisfaction. More importantly, they must prioritize these processes based on their impact and feasibility, ensuring that the organization is working on the right problems at the right time.

One of the most critical contributions of business teams is defining end-to-end requirements. They must think holistically—not just about their specific department but about how the proposed solution will fit into the larger organizational framework. For example, when the Sales team proposes a digital lead management tool, they must consider how it integrates with Credit for approval workflows, Operations for account opening, and Compliance for regulatory checks. Such cross-functional thinking ensures the solution is robust and aligned with the organization's goals.

However, one of the biggest challenges today is that many business teams work in silos. Each department focuses on its own pain points, often overlooking the broader organizational needs. This fragmented approach can lead to incomplete solutions, delays in implementation, and sometimes even failure of digital initiatives. To truly succeed, the mindset of "us versus them" must be replaced with a culture of collaboration.

Collaborative thinking is the cornerstone of successful digital transformation. When business teams come together, share insights, and co-create solutions with the technology department, the results are transformative. It ensures that the solutions are not just technologically advanced but also practical, user-friendly, and impactful across the organization.

Digital transformation is not just about new applications or tools—it is about a new way of working. And for that to happen, the business teams must lead the way by embracing collaboration, fostering a shared vision, and taking ownership of their role in this journey.

4.2.1. The Responsibility of Business in Driving Digital Initiatives

The success of any digital initiative hinges on the active and strategic involvement of business teams. While the technology team may design and implement solutions, it is the business teams that shape the direction, priorities, and functionality of these initiatives. Their role is not passive; they are co-creators and custodians of change, driving the transformation from ideation to execution.

At the core of their responsibility is business ownership. Digital transformation is not an IT project; it is a business-led endeavour. Business teams must own the outcomes and not merely delegate the execution to the technology department. This means defining clear goals, setting measurable success criteria, and ensuring that the digital initiative aligns with the organization's strategic objectives.

Another critical aspect is processing expertise. Business teams are the custodians of the operational workflows, customer journeys, and compliance requirements that define the organization. Their intimate understanding of these processes is invaluable when identifying areas ripe for improvement or automation. It is their responsibility to document these processes comprehensively and highlight pain points, inefficiencies, or risks that need addressing.

Change leadership is another key role. As the champions of transformation, business teams must communicate the purpose and benefits of digital initiatives to their colleagues, helping to build consensus and reduce resistance. They must foster an environment where change is embraced as an opportunity, not feared as a threat.

Additionally, business teams play a pivotal role in bridging the gap between strategy and execution. While the leadership may outline a vision for digital transformation, and IT may deliver the tools, business teams are the ones ensuring that these tools are practical, relevant, and integrated into daily operations. They must test, validate, and refine solutions to ensure they meet real-world needs.

Finally, the business teams are responsible for continuous improvement. Digital transformation is not a one-time event but an ongoing process. Business teams must regularly evaluate the impact of digital solutions, gather feedback, and identify areas for enhancement. Their commitment to iterative improvement ensures that the transformation remains dynamic and aligned with evolving business goals.

In essence, business teams are the torchbearers of digital transformation, translating strategy into actionable initiatives, ensuring alignment across functions, and fostering a culture of continuous progress.

4.2.2. Is Digitization Being Only a Management Wish?

One of the most pervasive challenges in digital transformation is the belief among employees that such initiatives are merely "management's wish." This mindset creates a passive approach to projects, where teams see digitization as something they are forced to comply with rather than actively embrace. Such a perspective not only undermines the spirit of transformation but also significantly hinders the potential for meaningful change.

The reality is that digital transformation is not a vanity project driven by the whims of leadership. It is a necessity for organizational survival and growth in today's highly competitive and fast-evolving world. Yet, in many banks and NBFCs, the drive for digitization is top-down. While this can provide a strategic push, it often results in employees viewing these initiatives as distant, disconnected, or irrelevant to their day-to-day work.

To break this mindset, a cultural shift is essential. Teams across business verticals must recognize that digital transformation is not just a management agenda but a shared organizational goal. It is about creating smarter, more efficient ways of working that benefit everyone—from frontline employees to customers and shareholders.

One practical step to achieve this is embedding digital transformation into the Key Result Areas (KRAs) of every business vertical. When digital initiatives become an integral part of an individual's performance metrics, it underscores their importance and ensures accountability. Employees should not only be participants in these projects but also take ownership of their success.

Equally important is the need for employees to devote quality time and effort to these projects. Transformation cannot happen in isolation or as an afterthought to the "real work." Business teams must adopt an organization-first mindset, dedicating their expertise, insights, and energy selflessly to the initiatives. This approach requires a shift from thinking, "How does this benefit me?" to "How does this strengthen the organization as a whole?"

Moreover, leadership has a crucial role in bridging the gap between top-down mandates and ground-level execution. They must communicate the "why" behind every project—how it aligns with the organization's vision, solves real problems, and creates value for all stakeholders. This ensures that employees see these initiatives not as an imposition but as an opportunity to contribute to the organization's success.

Finally, organizations need to foster a sense of pride and ownership in digital transformation. Success stories should be celebrated, and contributions recognized, no matter how small. When employees see the tangible outcomes of their efforts—faster processes, happier customers, or reduced workloads—they start to realize that digitization is not just management's wish but a collective win for the organization.

In short, overcoming this mindset is about creating alignment and accountability at all levels. Digital transformation is everyone's responsibility, and only through shared ownership and commitment can it truly succeed.

4.3. Processes for Business to Adopt Digital Transformation

Digital transformation is not just about adopting new technology, it's about transforming how an organization works, collaborates, and delivers value. For business teams, this requires a clear and structured approach. Below is a simplified model that any business team can adopt to plan, prioritize, drive, monitor, and measure the success of digital transformation projects.

4.3.1. Planning for Change: Setting the Foundation

Digital transformation begins with understanding the "why." The first step is for business teams to align on the organization's goals and how their specific function contributes to those goals. Here's how to plan effectively:

- **Define Clear Objectives:** What does success look like for your function? For example, faster customer onboarding, error-free processes, or improved compliance.

- **Assess Current Processes:** Identify gaps in your existing workflows. What is slowing you down? What frustrates your team or your customers?

- **Engage Stakeholders Early:** Bring everyone impacted by the transformation—across sales, credit, operations, collections, and legal—into the conversation. Change is less daunting when people feel included from the start.

4.3.2. Prioritizing What to Transform

With endless possibilities for digitization, it's essential to focus on what matters most. Use this simple prioritization framework:

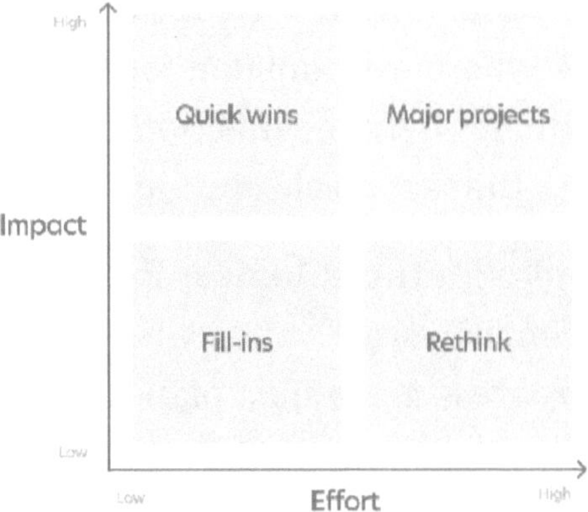

- **Impact vs. Effort Matrix:** Evaluate projects based on their potential business impact (revenue growth, cost savings, risk reduction) versus the effort required (time, resources, complexity).

- **Customer-Centric Thinking:** Prioritize processes that directly improve the customer experience. A happy customer is the best ROI.

- **Quick Wins vs. Strategic Goals:** Balance quick, visible wins that boost morale with long-term transformational projects that drive sustained value.

4.3.3. Driving the Projects: From Vision to Execution

Once priorities are set, the focus shifts to execution. Business teams should follow a structured project management approach:

- **Create a Cross-Functional Task Force:** Include representatives from every function impacted by the project. Collaborative thinking ensures no blind spots in the solution design.

- **Define Roles and Responsibilities:** Clearly articulate who is responsible for what. For example, business teams own the functional requirements, and IT delivers the technical solution.

- **Adopt Agile Methodologies:** Break the project into smaller, manageable phases (sprints). Regularly review progress and adjust plans based on feedback.

- **Communicate Continuously:** Keep all stakeholders updated on the project's goals, milestones, and progress. Transparency reduces resistance and builds trust.

4.3.4. Monitoring and Reporting Progress

Digital transformation projects require active tracking to ensure they stay on course:

- **Establish Key Performance Indicators (KPIs):** Define measurable outcomes for each project. For example, "Reduce loan processing time by 50%" or "Achieve 99% accuracy in reconciliations."

- **Use Project Management Tools:** Leverage tools like Jira, Trello, or Asana for task tracking and status updates.

- **Conduct Regular Reviews:** Weekly or bi-weekly check-ins help address bottlenecks early and keep momentum high.

- **Gather Feedback Continuously:** Create feedback loops with end-users to ensure the solution is practical and meets their needs.

4.3.5. Measuring Success: Beyond Go-Live

The real measure of success isn't just launching a digital project—it's ensuring it delivers sustained value. Here's how to measure:

- **Compare Before and After Metrics:** Did the process improve? For instance, measure reduced processing times, increased customer satisfaction scores, or cost savings.

- **Check Adoption Rates:** Are employees and customers actually using the new system? Low adoption often signals the need for additional training or tweaks.

- **Evaluate Business Impact:** Did the project achieve its intended outcomes? Was there a measurable return on investment (ROI)?

- **Celebrate Wins:** Recognize team efforts and celebrate milestones, no matter how small. Positive reinforcement drives future engagement.

A Simplified Framework for Business Teams

1. **Plan:** Understand the "why" and define goals.

2. **Prioritize:** Focus on high-impact, customer-centric changes.

3. **Drive:** Build cross-functional teams and execute with agility.

4. **Monitor:** Track progress and address roadblocks in real-time.

5. **Measure:** Assess adoption, impact, and ROI post-implementation.

By following this structured yet flexible approach, business teams can not only align with the organization's digital vision but also take ownership of its success. Remember, digital transformation is not a sprint—it's a marathon requiring collaboration, commitment, and a shared sense of purpose.

4.4. Real-Life Experiences: Successes & Challenges

No digital transformation journey is without its highs and lows. While some projects achieve timely success and deliver immense value, others face delays, roadblocks, or even fail to meet expectations. These experiences provide invaluable lessons on what to do—and what to avoid—in future initiatives.

Projects That Went Live Successfully on Time

1. **Automated Loan Origination System**

    o **Objective:** To reduce loan approval time from days to hours, providing customers with instant loan decisions.

    o **Why It Worked:**

        o Clear objectives were set by the business team, and IT was given detailed, end-to-end functional requirements.

        o Strong collaboration between credit, operations, and technology teams ensured no gaps in the process.

- Agile methodology enabled incremental delivery, with feedback from pilot users incorporated into the solution.

- **Outcome:** Loan approvals were streamlined, leading to increased customer satisfaction and a 30% growth in loan disbursements within six months of implementation.

2. **Customer Self-Service Portal**

- **Objective:** To empower customers to manage their accounts, payments, and service requests online.

- **Why It Worked:**

  - The business team identified key pain points for customers and prioritized features accordingly.

  - Extensive employee and customer training led to high adoption rates post-launch.

  - **Outcome:** Reduced branch footfall by 40%, freeing up staff for higher-value tasks and improving customer satisfaction scores.

CRM Project Success: A Case Study of Timely Execution

Project Objective: To implement a comprehensive Customer Relationship Management (CRM) system that enables seamless customer interactions, tracks the customer journey, and enhances cross-sell opportunities in one of the leading NBFCs.

Timeline: The project was planned for a six-month delivery and went live successfully as scheduled, demonstrating exemplary execution.

Key Success Metrics

1. **Active Business Involvement:**

   - The business teams (sales, credit, collections, and operations) were deeply involved from day one, identifying pain points and defining clear objectives.

   - End-to-end requirements were outlined collaboratively, ensuring that the CRM was tailored to the NBFC's unique needs.

- o   Business stakeholders participated in regular sprint reviews to validate functionalities, preventing rework and ensuring alignment with goals.

- o   **Impact:** Enhanced ownership and a 100% alignment of the solution with user needs.

2. **On-Time Approvals:**

- o   A steering committee comprising senior management and cross-functional leaders was set up to ensure expedited decision-making.

- o   Approval workflows were predefined, avoiding unnecessary delays.

- o   Escalation mechanisms ensured that any roadblocks were promptly addressed at the appropriate level.

3. **Cross-Functional Collaboration:**

- o   A project team with representatives from IT, business, legal, compliance, and audit worked cohesively, fostering a sense of shared accountability.

- o   Weekly progress reviews encouraged transparent communication, aligning all stakeholders on the same page.

- o   Any cross-functional dependencies were proactively identified and resolved through joint workshops.

- o **Impact:** Reduced bottlenecks and seamless integration of the CRM with other systems, such as loan origination and customer service platforms.

4. **Agile Execution:**

   - o The project adopted an agile methodology, with deliverables broken into two-week sprints.

   - o Pilot rollouts allowed user feedback to be incorporated early, ensuring a refined and user-friendly final product.

   - o **Impact:** The phased approach minimized risks and ensured a smooth go-live experience.

Outcome:

- **Improved Customer Engagement:** The CRM enabled a 25% improvement in customer query resolution times and a 30% increase in cross-sell conversion rates within three months of implementation.

- **Higher Productivity:** Sales and support teams reported a 40% reduction in time spent on manual tasks, thanks to automation features in the CRM.

- **Organizational Impact:** The successful delivery boosted morale and trust between business and IT teams, setting the stage for future collaborative projects.

Key Takeaway: The success of this CRM project underscores the importance of business involvement, timely decision-making, and cross-functional collaboration. It demonstrates that with the right alignment and commitment, even ambitious projects can be delivered on time, driving tangible value for the organization.

Projects That Faced Delays or Were Scrapped

Case Study of a Loan Origination System (LOS) Implementation: Lessons from Adoption Challenges

Project Background: Two years before I took over, a Loan Origination System (LOS) was implemented to streamline the credit process from login to disbursal. While the system was technically sound and aligned with the organization's initial requirements, it faced significant resistance from the business team, resulting in minimal adoption.

Key Challenges Faced

1. **Regulatory and Business Process Changes Post-Go-Live:**

    o   Over the two years, regulatory updates and evolving business priorities led to several changes in the credit process.

    o   These changes were not initially reflected in the LOS, causing a perceived misalignment between the system's functionality and the current operational needs.

2. **Resistance from Business Teams (Credit):**

    o   The credit team had become accustomed to their manual and email-driven workflows, leading to an inherent resistance to adopt a digital system.

- o Feedback from the team was vague, with comments like "the solution doesn't match our process," but without measurable or specific gaps identified.

- o This lack of clarity in feedback prolonged the evaluation and troubleshooting phase.

3. **Lack of System Familiarity:**

- o The team's unfamiliarity with the LOS and its capabilities contributed to their reluctance.

- o Manual processes were perceived as more "reliable," even though the LOS could achieve the same outcomes with greater efficiency.

Steps Taken to Address the Challenges

1. **Process Alignment and System Refinement:**

- o I conducted a detailed evaluation of the LOS and the current credit processes, mapping them against each other.

- o One by one, regulatory and business process updates were incorporated into the system to ensure alignment with current workflows.

2. **Live Case Demonstrations:**

- o To address the vague feedback, I organized sessions with the credit team and IT to run live cases in the LOS.

- o These sessions demonstrated that the system could handle the complete workflow—from login to disbursal—without any issues.

- o The goal was to bridge the gap between perceived and actual system capabilities.

3. **Engagement and Education:**

- o Regular workshops and hands-on training sessions were conducted to familiarize the credit team with the LOS.

- o By involving them in these demonstrations, I aimed to build trust in the system's functionality.

4. **Management Intervention:**

- o Despite all efforts, adoption remained a challenge due to entrenched manual habits.

- o Management intervention became crucial to emphasize the strategic importance of the LOS and to mandate its use.

Outcome:

- **Adoption Achieved Under Pressure:** After extensive efforts and management directives, the credit team began using the LOS.

- **Lessons Learned:**

- o **Change Management Is Key:** Technology adoption isn't just about implementing the right solution; it's about managing people's mindset and processes.

- o **Continuous Engagement:** Business teams need to be continuously engaged, not just during the design phase but throughout the project lifecycle.

- o **Feedback Must Be Actionable:** Vague or unstructured feedback can delay progress. Clear, measurable inputs from business teams are critical.

- o **Leadership Support:** Management's active involvement is essential to overcome resistance and drive cultural change.

Key Takeaway: This experience highlights that resistance to change, rather than technical inadequacy, is often the biggest hurdle in digital transformation. While systems can be refined to meet evolving needs, fostering a culture of adoption and collaboration is vital to ensuring the success of any digital initiative.

Key Lessons from Successes and Failures

1. **Success Requires Shared Ownership:** Projects succeed when both business and IT teams take joint accountability for their success. Clear roles, open communication, and mutual respect are non-negotiable.

2. **Clarity Is Everything:** Success hinges on well-defined objectives and requirements. Ambiguity breeds inefficiency, rework, and frustration.

3. **User Acceptance Is Critical:** Resistance from end-users, whether due to fear of change or lack of training,

can derail even the best-planned initiatives. Early engagement and robust change management are key.

4. **Time Matters:** Delays are costly—not just in terms of money but also in terms of lost trust and momentum. Agile methodologies can help teams stay on track and adjust quickly to unforeseen challenges.

5. **Leadership Commitment:** Projects need unwavering support from leadership. Frequent leadership changes or lack of engagement can cause projects to lose direction.

Sharing these stories, with the specifics of what worked and what didn't, will inspire teams to approach digital transformation with a mindset of learning, collaboration, and resilience. It's a journey with many hurdles, but when tackled with the right strategies, it can yield transformative results.

Recommendation for Business Teams on Approaching Digital Transformation

Digital transformation is more than just a buzzword, it is a journey that redefines how organizations function, serve customers, and remain competitive. For business teams, this journey is a shared responsibility that requires commitment, clarity, and collaboration.

Here are key takeaways for approaching digital transformation effectively:

1. **Adopt a Business-First Mindset:** Understand that digital transformation is not just an IT initiative; it's a

business imperative. The success of any digital project hinges on the business team's ability to articulate clear, end-to-end requirements, aligning them with organizational goals.

2. **Foster a Culture of Collaboration:** No process starts and ends within a single team. Digital transformation demands breaking silos and fostering collaboration across sales, credit, operations, collections, legal, compliance, and audit. Unified efforts are the foundation of seamless and sustainable change.

3. **Prioritize with Purpose:** Not every process can or should be digitized at once. Focus on areas with the highest impact on efficiency, customer experience, and profitability. Use data-driven decision-making to identify what deserves priority and ensure all stakeholders are aligned.

4. **Lead Change, Don't Resist It:** Transformation often comes with discomfort and disruption. Instead of resisting change, embrace it as an opportunity to innovate. Be open to new ways of working, and remember that the initial learning curve is temporary, but the benefits are lasting.

5. **Take Ownership of the Process:** Digital transformation is not just a management wish—it is an organizational responsibility. Business teams should have it as part of their KRAs to actively participate in projects, give timely approvals, and ensure the solutions delivered are aligned with real-world requirements.

6. **Invest in Adoption:** A well-designed system is only as good as its users. Ensure that team members are trained and equipped to use new systems effectively. Adoption is not a one-time event; it requires consistent effort, feedback, and leadership support.

7. **Measure Success and Celebrate Wins:** Define clear success metrics for each digital initiative—be it efficiency gains, customer satisfaction, or cost reductions. Monitor progress regularly and celebrate milestones to build momentum and reinforce the value of transformation.

8. **Commit to Continuous Improvement:** Digital transformation isn't a destination—it's an evolving journey. Stay agile and be ready to adapt processes and systems as customer expectations, regulatory requirements, and market dynamics change.

Final Thought: For business teams, digital transformation is an opportunity to lead the way, not just follow instructions. By taking ownership, collaborating effectively, and approaching every project with an "organization-first" mindset, you can drive meaningful change that benefits the business, its customers, and the industry at large. Transformation begins when everyone sees themselves as a part of the solution.

"Change is the end result of all true learning."

– Leo Buscaglia

05

THE TECHNICAL CHALLENGE: ROLE OF IT

IT plays an indispensable role in driving digital transformation, acting as the bridge between business vision and technological execution. However, despite being at the centre of this evolution, IT often faces significant challenges that can derail progress. Some of these hurdles are technical, such as legacy systems or resource limitations, but others stem from people, mindsets, and organizational culture. Understanding and addressing these challenges is crucial for IT to fulfil its role as a strategic partner in transformation.

5.1. Role of IT in Transformation

5.1.1. The Partnership Between Business and IT

Successful digital transformation requires IT to work hand-in-hand with business teams. IT must translate business needs into technical solutions, while business teams must clearly articulate their requirements. However, this partnership often falters due to:

- **Business Perspective:** Business teams often prioritize speed, market readiness, and achieving tangible results. Their focus is on customer satisfaction, faster go-to-market strategies, and immediate operational benefits.

- o **IT Perspective:** IT teams, on the other hand, emphasize feasibility, scalability, and security. They are responsible for building systems that are robust, compliant, and capable of supporting long-term goals.

This divergence can result in delays, friction, and even failed initiatives when each side feels their priorities are overlooked.

Mitigation Strategies:

1. **Joint Prioritization Workshops:**

   - o Schedule regular collaborative sessions where IT and business leaders jointly discuss project priorities and trade-offs.

   - o Use frameworks like the **MoSCoW method (Must have, should have, Could have, Won't have)** to determine shared priorities.

2. **Agile Methodology:**

   - o Implement Agile practices such as Scrum or Kanban, where IT and business teams work in short, iterative sprints with shared goals and regular feedback loops.

   - o This keeps projects aligned with evolving business needs while ensuring technical feasibility.

3. **Establish a Governance Board**:

   o   Create a cross-functional governance board comprising representatives from IT, business, compliance, and other key stakeholders.

   o   This board can oversee project progress, resolve conflicts, and ensure alignment of priorities.

4. **KPIs that Reflect Shared Goals**:

   o   Define success metrics that combine business outcomes (e.g., revenue growth, customer satisfaction) with IT goals (e.g., system uptime, cybersecurity compliance).

   o   Shared accountability fosters alignment.

5.2. Shifting the Mindset: IT as a Strategic Partner

To overcome this mindset, IT must reposition itself as an enabler of growth and profitability. This requires a deliberate effort to highlight IT's contributions, align with business goals, and demonstrate its impact on the bottom line.

5.2.1. Showcase IT's Value Beyond Cost Savings

IT teams must move beyond presenting their contributions solely in terms of cost reduction. Instead, they should emphasize:

- **Revenue Generation**: For example, implementing a customer relationship management (CRM) system that drives cross-selling and upselling.

- **Customer Retention**: Show how improved user experiences and streamlined processes reduce churn.

- **Market Expansion**: Demonstrate how digital platforms enable businesses to enter new markets or scale operations.

5.2.2. Share Success Stories

Storytelling is a powerful way to reshape perceptions. Real-life examples of IT-driven success can help business leaders see the department as a driver of growth. Examples include:

- **Automation Reducing Loan Processing Times**: A financial institution may highlight how IT-led automation reduced loan processing times from days to hours, directly improving customer satisfaction and increasing loan disbursals.

- **Data Analytics Enhancing Revenue**: Demonstrate how advanced analytics enabled precision targeting for marketing campaigns, driving up cross-selling opportunities.

- **Cloud Migration Reducing Costs**: Transitioning to cloud-based systems not only reduces infrastructure costs but also improves agility and scalability.

5.2.3. Align IT Goals with Business Objectives

IT teams must work closely with business leaders to ensure their initiatives align with organizational goals. This includes:

- **Proactively Addressing Business Needs**: Collaborating with business teams to identify pain points and design solutions that directly impact revenue or efficiency.

- **Participating in Strategy Discussions**: Ensuring IT leadership has a seat at the table during strategic planning, allowing them to influence decisions with technology insights.

5.3. IT as a Profit Center

Positioning IT as a profit center involves demonstrating how IT investments yield returns. IT is no longer just about maintaining infrastructure; it is about building capabilities that drive growth.

5.3.1. IT as a Growth Enabler

- **Digital Products**: Developing customer-facing digital applications, such as mobile apps or online portals, that create new revenue streams.

- **Data-Driven Decision-Making**: Using advanced analytics to unlock business insights, improving forecasting, and optimizing operations.

- **Scalable Infrastructure**: Implementing flexible, scalable systems that support rapid growth without exponential cost increases.

5.3.2. IT as a Problem-Solver

- **Process Optimization**: Automating repetitive tasks, improving operational efficiency, and freeing up resources for strategic initiatives.

- **Cybersecurity**: Protecting the organization from costly breaches and ensuring customer trust in digital channels.

- **Regulatory Compliance**: Building systems that simplify compliance, reducing risk and saving on penalties or reputational damage.

5.4. Practical Steps to Drive the Mindset Change

5.4.1. Communicate the ROI of IT Investments

- Break down IT projects into tangible business outcomes. For example:

  - An investment in automation may reduce operational costs by 20%.

  - A new digital lending platform may increase disbursals by 30% in the first year.

- Present IT initiatives in business language, focusing on value rather than technical specifications.

5.4.2. Create IT-Business Partnerships

- Embed IT leaders within business teams to foster collaboration and ensure alignment.

- Use cross-functional governance boards to prioritize projects and measure their impact collectively.

5.4.3. Build a Culture of Innovation

- Foster an environment where IT is encouraged to experiment and innovate.

- Reward both IT and business teams for collaborative successes in digital initiatives.

5.4.4. Measure and Report Success

- Develop clear metrics for IT contributions, such as:

  - Revenue impact of new platforms.

  - Reduction in customer complaints due to system improvements.

  - Time savings from automation projects.

- Share regular updates with leadership and employees to reinforce IT's strategic role.

Overcoming the "IT as a cost center" mindset is essential for organizations that want to stay competitive in the digital age. IT is no longer just a support function—it is a profit center, an innovation driver, and a key enabler of business growth. By showcasing its contributions, aligning with business goals, and demonstrating tangible value, IT can firmly establish itself as a strategic partner that is indispensable to the organization's success.

06

THE CULTURAL CHALLENGE: PEOPLE AND RESISTANCE IN IT

One of the most significant roadblocks in digital transformation isn't the technology itself; it's the people—their mindsets, their resistance to change, and the cultural barriers within the IT ecosystem. This is particularly evident in the IT vertical, Business Solutions Groups, and Business IT teams. Despite their critical role in transformation, these teams often operate with certain ingrained behaviours and attitudes that can hinder progress.

Let's delve into the challenges, mindsets, and how these can be addressed effectively while maintaining IT governance and security standards.

6.1. Current Challenges in IT Culture

6.1.1. The Overcomplication of Processes

Many IT teams inadvertently overcomplicate processes, often magnifying efforts and deliverables. This behaviour can stem from a belief that the inherently complex nature of IT requires extensive layers of quality checks and compliance measures. The use of technical jargon and abbreviations further exacerbates the issue, alienating business teams and widening the gap between IT and business alignment. Additionally, there is sometimes an unconscious tendency among IT personnel to overstate the complexity of their work to justify extended timelines, resource demands, or budget increases. While usually unintentional, these practices can create a perception of IT as a slow, bureaucratic function, frustrating business teams and delaying project progress.

- **IT is complex by nature**: Teams believe their work requires layers of processes to ensure quality and compliance, making it difficult for business leaders to comprehend.

- **Technical jargon creates a barrier**: Acronyms, abbreviations, and overly technical explanations often alienate business teams, creating a divide between IT and business.

- **Effort justification**: Some IT personnel unconsciously overstate the complexity of their work to justify extended timelines or additional resources.

To address this, IT teams need to adopt a culture of clarity and collaboration. Processes should be designed to balance thoroughness with efficiency, ensuring that quality and compliance are maintained without unnecessary layers of complexity. Communication is key—IT teams should prioritize using simple, business-friendly language to explain projects, minimizing technical jargon and focusing on tangible outcomes. Regular workshops and collaborative sessions between IT and business teams can help bridge understanding and create shared ownership of deliverables.

Additionally, IT leaders should promote a culture of transparency by documenting processes, setting realistic timelines, and regularly sharing updates with business stakeholders. Establishing clear Service Level Agreements (SLAs) and adhering to them helps build trust and demonstrates IT's commitment to efficiency. When IT shifts from being a perceived bottleneck to a collaborative enabler, it not only streamlines operations but also strengthens its role as a strategic partner in driving transformation.

6.1.2. Resistance to Simplification

Simplifying IT processes and communication often encounters internal resistance, driven by deeply rooted fears and concerns within IT teams. A fear of losing control is common, as teams worry that streamlined processes may reduce their authority or compromise the thoroughness required in their work. Attachment to long-established methods further hinders progress, as these processes are often seen as tried-and-tested practices. Additionally, legitimate concerns about maintaining IT General Controls (ITGC) and security measures contribute to a reluctance to simplify workflows. This resistance, though understandable, can lead to inefficiencies, strained relationships with business teams, and slower progress in digital transformation initiatives.

- **Fear of Losing Control**: IT teams may fear that simplifying processes will dilute their authority or compromise the thoroughness of their work.

- **Attachment to Established Methods**: Long-standing processes and systems are often deeply ingrained, making change difficult.

- **Security Concerns**: IT teams are rightfully cautious about compromising ITGC (IT General Controls) and security processes, leading to a preference for more complex and rigid workflows.

Gradual and Collaborative Simplification

Overcoming resistance to simplification requires a balanced approach that respects IT concerns while fostering trust and collaboration. IT leaders should initiate change by involving teams in workshops and discussions that demonstrate how simplification enhances efficiency without compromising quality or security. Clearly outlining non-negotiable controls, such as ITGC and security measures, ensures that essential safeguards are maintained while allowing for flexibility in other areas.

To ease the transition, changes should be introduced incrementally, starting with small wins that highlight the benefits of simplification. For instance, adopting collaborative tools that streamline communication between IT and business teams can quickly show value without significant disruption. Additionally, fostering a culture of empowerment—where team members are encouraged to innovate and refine processes—helps build confidence in the shift toward simplification.

6.1.3. Lack of Transparency and Accountability

To address these issues, IT teams should implement mechanisms for clear communication and accountability. Developing and adhering to SLAs provides measurable benchmarks for IT performance, setting expectations for response times, project timelines, and deliverables. Regularly scheduled reporting, including progress updates, challenges, and timelines, fosters transparency and builds trust with business leaders.

- **Opaque Processes**: Many business leaders feel left in the dark about IT workflows, priorities, and project timelines.

- **Absence of SLAs**: Without clearly defined Service Level Agreements (SLAs), business teams may perceive IT as unaccountable or unresponsive.

- **Limited Reporting**: A lack of regular reporting on IT performance, timelines, and challenges prevents open dialogue and collaboration.

IT teams can adopt dashboards and project management tools that allow business stakeholders to track progress in real-time. This transparency encourages collaboration and ensures that business teams are aware of priorities and constraints. Finally, fostering a culture of accountability within IT, where team members take ownership of their deliverables and timelines, reinforces trust and strengthens the partnership between IT and business.

6.1.4. Mindset of "We Know Better"

In some organizations, IT professionals adopt a mindset where they believe they inherently understand business needs better than the business teams themselves. While this confidence may stem from technical expertise and exposure to cross-functional workflows, it can lead to communication barriers and one-sided decision-making. Business inputs may be dismissed or undervalued, creating friction and a sense of exclusion among stakeholders. This siloed approach results in solutions that may not align with actual business needs, leading to misaligned deliverables, underutilized systems, and missed opportunities for value creation.

- **Communication Barriers**: IT may dismiss input from business teams, leading to friction and misaligned deliverables.

- **One-Sided Decision-Making**: IT solutions are often developed in silos without adequate input from business stakeholders, resulting in suboptimal outcomes.

Cultivating a Collaborative Mindset

To address this challenge, IT leaders must foster a culture of partnership and humility within their teams. This begins with acknowledging the domain expertise of business teams and creating structured forums for their input during every stage of the project lifecycle. Regular joint workshops, requirement-gathering sessions, and validation checkpoints can ensure that business needs are clearly understood and reflected in the solution.

IT teams should also adopt agile methodologies, where iterative feedback loops allow business stakeholders to review and refine deliverables in real-time. This ensures that the end product aligns with expectations and fosters a sense of ownership among business teams. Encouraging IT professionals to shadow business processes or participate in frontline operations can further enhance their understanding of on-the-ground challenges, reducing assumptions and fostering mutual respect. By embracing collaboration, IT can deliver solutions that are both technically robust and strategically aligned with business goals.

Collaboration is the Key for Success...

6.2. Recommendations to Overcome IT Cultural Challenges

6.2.1. Simplify and Streamline Processes

IT leaders should focus on creating a balance between thoroughness and efficiency by:

- **Designing Transparent Workflows**: Develop simple, well-documented processes that are easy for business leaders to follow and understand.

- **Reducing Complexity Without Compromising Security**: Use automation and smart tools to ensure compliance with ITGC and security protocols while simplifying processes.

- **Encouraging Open Collaboration**: Involve business teams in process design to ensure their needs are considered and processes are intuitive for non-technical stakeholders.

6.2.2. Introduce SLAs and Regular Reporting

Accountability and transparency can transform IT's relationship with the business.

- **Set Clear SLAs**: Define specific, measurable timelines for every IT process, such as ticket resolution, system updates, and project milestones.

- **Report Performance**: Share monthly SLA reports with business leaders, highlighting achievements and addressing delays with clear explanations.

- **Establish Feedback Mechanisms**: Use regular reviews with business teams to gather input and identify opportunities for improvement.

6.2.3. Humanize IT Communication

IT leaders must break down technical jargon and foster better communication by:

- **Using Business Language**: Translate IT concepts into terms that align with business goals and strategies.

- **Providing Training**: Offer cross-functional training to help IT teams understand business processes and vice versa.

- **Appointing Translators**: Assign Business IT liaisons who can bridge the gap between technical teams and business leaders.

6.2.4. Foster a Culture of Collaboration

- **Involve IT in Business Strategy**: Invite IT leaders to participate in strategic business discussions to create a shared sense of ownership.

- **Encourage Cross-Functional Teams**: Pair IT and business professionals to work together on projects, fostering mutual understanding and respect.

- **Celebrate Shared Successes**: Highlight collaborative wins to reinforce the value of teamwork and partnership.

6.2.5. Shift from "We Know Better" to "We Solve Together"

IT leaders must encourage a mindset of partnership within their teams.

- **Adopt a Service-Oriented Approach**: Encourage IT to see themselves as solution providers rather than gatekeepers.

- **Encourage Curiosity and Empathy**: Train IT teams to ask questions, listen to business concerns, and approach problems with a collaborative spirit.

- **Measure Adoption Success**: Evaluate IT's success based on how well solutions are adopted and utilized by the business, not just on technical implementation.

The cultural challenges within IT, Business Solutions Groups, and Business IT are not insurmountable, but they require intentional efforts to address. By simplifying processes, improving transparency, and fostering collaboration, IT teams can become trusted partners to the business. A culture of mutual respect, shared goals, and clear communication is the foundation of successful digital transformation. For IT, this means moving beyond technical excellence to embrace a human-centered approach that delivers true value to the organization

6.3. Navigating the Paradox

Embarking on a digital transformation journey is both exciting and challenging. While the promise of innovation and efficiency is alluring, organizations often encounter several obstacles along the way. Let's explore these challenges, learn from success stories, and outline strategies for business and IT leaders to navigate this complex landscape together.

Common Roadblocks in Digital Transformation

Cultural Barriers: Resistance to change is a significant hurdle. Employees accustomed to traditional workflows may be hesitant to adopt new technologies, fearing job displacement or the unknown. This reluctance can stall transformation efforts and impede progress.

Technical Challenges: Legacy systems, often deeply embedded in an organization's operations, can be difficult to integrate with modern technologies. The complexity of these outdated systems can lead to increased costs and extended timelines during the transformation process.

Strategic Misalignment: Without a clear, unified vision, digital initiatives can become fragmented. Misalignment between business objectives and IT capabilities can result in projects that fail to deliver expected outcomes, wasting resources and diminishing morale.

"A problem well-defined is a problem half-solved."

– Charles Kettering

07

BUILDING A FRAMEWORK FOR MANAGING DIGITAL TRANSFORMATION

Digital transformation in banking is not a one-off initiative but a continuous journey that requires a clear, structured framework. This framework ensures alignment between business and IT, while fostering collaboration, accountability, and efficiency across teams. A well-defined framework serves as a roadmap to navigate complexities, prioritize efforts, and deliver impactful outcomes. It involves identifying transformation opportunities through benchmarking, evaluating solutions with a blend of functional and technical perspectives, justifying investments with a strong business case, and ensuring robust project governance.

While some points in this session may seem repetitive, this repetition is intentional to emphasize critical takeaways and reinforce the importance of a structured approach to managing transformation. A robust framework is the backbone of any successful digital initiative, enabling banks to stay agile and competitive in a rapidly evolving industry. By setting clear evaluation criteria, forming empowered transformation councils, and implementing effective project controls, banks can overcome common roadblocks and drive meaningful change. This reiteration underscores the need for disciplined execution, transparent communication, and cross-functional collaboration at every stage of the transformation journey.

Building this framework is not just about delivering projects on time but ensuring they add long-term value to the organization. It's about empowering teams with the tools, processes, and authority to succeed while fostering a culture of innovation and adaptability.

7.1. Identifying Opportunities for Transformation

The first step in digital transformation is recognizing where change is needed. This involves assessing existing processes across departments like Sales, Credit, Operations, Collections, and Compliance to identify inefficiencies, bottlenecks, or gaps that hinder performance or customer experience. Opportunities for transformation often lie in areas with repetitive tasks, manual interventions, and high error rates.

A structured approach includes benchmarking processes against industry leaders, customer feedback analysis, and evaluating regulatory changes that demand process reengineering. Prioritizing opportunities with the greatest impact on business growth, operational efficiency, or customer satisfaction ensures a focused transformation strategy. Identifying these areas sets the foundation for meaningful and sustainable digital initiatives.

Evaluation Criteria for Digitization

1. **Departmental Needs Assessment**: Each department—Sales, Credit, Collections, Compliance, Operations—must identify processes ripe for digitization based on pain points, inefficiencies, and regulatory needs.

2. **Customer-Centric Focus**: Prioritize transformations that enhance customer experiences or reduce turnaround times.

3. **Benchmarking**: Use industry data or case studies to compare processes with leading banks to identify gaps and improvement opportunities.

Template for Benchmarking: A simple benchmarking template can include:

- **Process Name**

- **Current Metrics (e.g., TAT, cost)**

- **Industry Best Metrics**

- **Gap Analysis**

- **Action Plan**

Evaluating Vendors and Solutions

Selecting the right vendor or solution is critical to the success of any digital transformation initiative. Business teams should focus on the functional fit of the solution, ensuring it aligns with the specific needs and goals of the process being transformed. Meanwhile, IT teams should evaluate technical aspects like scalability, security, and compatibility with existing systems. Vendor credibility, support infrastructure, and the ability to customize the solution are equally important. A collaborative evaluation process involving both business and IT ensures a balanced decision that meets functional and technical requirements while delivering maximum value for the organization.

a. **Market Assessment**

- The business team should research multiple vendors or solutions based on functionality, cost, scalability, and ease of use.

- Engage IT early to assess technical feasibility and compatibility with existing systems.

b. **Functional and Technical Evaluation**

- Business teams should focus on user-friendliness, relevance to business needs, and ROI.

- IT evaluates the solution's security, integration capabilities, and scalability.

Template for Vendor Evaluation:

- **Criteria**: Functional fit, technical compatibility, vendor track record, cost, support model.

- **Weightage**: Assign weights to each criterion based on priority.

- **Scoring**: Use a scoring system to rank vendors objectively.

Building a Strong Business Case

Creating a compelling business case is the cornerstone of initiating any digital transformation project. For business teams, this involves identifying the tangible and intangible benefits of the proposed transformation and articulating them in a manner that resonates with decision-makers. Start by clearly defining the problem or opportunity the transformation aims to address, such as improving customer experience, reducing operational inefficiencies, or complying with regulatory changes. Quantify the expected benefits, whether it's a reduction in processing time, cost savings, revenue growth, or enhanced customer satisfaction.

The business case should also include a cost-benefit analysis, factoring in the investment required for technology, vendor solutions, training, and potential disruption during implementation. Highlight the value proposition by aligning the project's objectives with the organization's strategic goals. Additionally, outline risks and mitigation strategies to demonstrate a realistic and well-rounded understanding of the project scope. Finally, emphasize the importance of cross-functional collaboration, as successful digital transformation is not just about technology but also about driving cultural and operational change. By presenting a clear, data-backed, and goal-oriented business case, business teams can secure management buy-in and build momentum for impactful transformation initiatives.

Cost Justification and Value Proposition

Business teams must develop a compelling business case that includes:

- The projected benefits (e.g., cost savings, efficiency, customer satisfaction).

- The estimated costs of implementation, training, and ongoing maintenance.

- A clear ROI analysis to convince management.

Forming a Transformation Council

A Transformation Council is essential for steering digital initiatives and ensuring their alignment with organizational goals. This council acts as a governance body, comprising key stakeholders from business, IT, compliance, and other relevant functions. Its primary role is to oversee the project's progress, resolve conflicts, and drive accountability. The council should include decision-makers with the authority to allocate resources and address roadblocks, as well as representatives from operational levels to bring practical insights.

The council ensures a balanced approach by blending strategic vision with functional expertise. It sets clear objectives, reviews milestones, monitors performance against key metrics, and ensures adherence to timelines. Regular meetings and structured reporting enable transparency and swift decision-making. Empowering the council to make critical decisions fosters agility and prevents bottlenecks, creating a culture of ownership and collaboration. A well-structured Transformation Council not only accelerates project delivery but also establishes a framework for sustaining innovation and continuous improvement.

Empowered Decision-Making

- A dedicated transformation council comprising cross-functional leaders ensures faster decision-making and accountability.

- The council must have a clear mandate and authority to approve changes, resolve conflicts, and ensure progress.

Review Mechanism

- Regular progress reviews with predefined metrics (e.g., milestone completion, budget adherence).

- Transparent reporting to stakeholders to maintain trust and momentum.

Techniques and Templates for Project Execution

Effective project execution in digital transformation requires a structured approach, underpinned by proven techniques and well-designed templates. Techniques such as Agile methodology foster flexibility, allowing teams to adapt to changes quickly, while the Waterfall model may be appropriate for projects with well-defined scopes and linear processes. Key templates include detailed project charters, stakeholder matrices, and risk management plans, ensuring clarity and alignment among all stakeholders.

Progress tracking tools, such as Gantt charts or Kanban boards, provide visibility into timelines and task dependencies, enabling proactive management of potential delays. Regular use of communication templates, like meeting minutes and status reports, ensures consistent updates and accountability. By combining these techniques with robust templates, organizations can streamline execution, maintain focus on objectives, and mitigate risks effectively.

Project Controls

- ○ **Scope Definition**: Clearly document the project scope to avoid scope creep.

- ○ **Timeline Management**: Use tools like Gantt charts or Agile boards for milestone tracking.

- ○ **Risk Assessment**: Identify potential risks early and plan mitigation strategies.

Governance Templates

- ○ **Progress Dashboards**: Provide an at-a-glance view of project health (e.g., on-track, at risk, delayed).

- ○ **SLA Templates**: Define clear service level agreements for each phase of the project.

- ○ **Issue Logs**: Maintain a centralized log of issues and their resolution status.

Driving Success through Accountability

Accountability is the cornerstone of success in any digital transformation initiative. It ensures that every team member, from business leaders to IT professionals, understands their role and takes ownership of their responsibilities. Clear delineation of tasks, along with defined timelines and measurable outcomes, fosters a culture of commitment. Regular progress reviews and transparent reporting mechanisms keep everyone aligned and motivated.

When accountability is embedded in the organizational ethos, it prevents finger-pointing and silos, driving collaborative problem-solving instead. Leadership plays a pivotal role by setting the tone, rewarding accountability, and addressing gaps promptly. By making accountability a non-negotiable principle, organizations create an environment where projects are executed with precision, challenges are addressed proactively, and goals are achieved consistently.

Empowering Teams

- Ensure that each team member or sub-team has clearly defined roles and responsibilities.

- Encourage open communication and collaboration between business and IT to reduce friction.

Regular Training

- Equip business teams with the skills to handle digital tools and evaluate project progress confidently.

The journey of digital transformation in banking is a multifaceted process that requires more than just technology; it demands a comprehensive framework built on collaboration, accountability, and strategic vision. This framework is not just a guide—it is a tool to navigate challenges, bridge gaps between business and IT, and deliver impactful outcomes that redefine organizational success.

By identifying opportunities for transformation, benchmarking processes with industry leaders, and meticulously evaluating vendors, banks can create a foundation that supports seamless and impactful digital initiatives. Establishing empowered transformation councils and leveraging structured templates and techniques for project execution ensures disciplined execution and sustained momentum.

The benefits of a robust framework are profound: enhanced customer experiences, streamlined operations, and a culture of accountability and innovation. It also fosters a forward-thinking mindset that embraces change as a pathway to growth, equipping organizations to stay agile and competitive in an evolving industry landscape.

Ultimately, this framework is about creating long-term value—value for customers through better services, value for employees through improved processes, and value for the organization through enhanced operational efficiency and strategic growth. With the right framework, digital transformation becomes more than a goal; it becomes a continuous journey of evolution and progress.

Drive to Success through Digital Transformation...

Customer-Centric Transformation

In the journey of digital transformation, customer-centricity must be at the heart of every decision and delivery. For IT teams within banks or financial institutions, business users are often viewed as the primary customers. However, we must not lose sight of the real end customer—the individuals and businesses that interact with the bank's products and services. Every transformation initiative should be driven by the ultimate goal of enhancing their experience.

The evolving expectations of customers in today's competitive world are both an opportunity and a challenge. Customers demand seamless, intuitive, and efficient experiences, whether they are accessing services digitally or visiting a branch. If a bank fails to meet these expectations, there is always a competitor ready to step in and solve the same need. This makes it critical for every transformation to start by empathizing with the customer—viewing the journey through their eyes and addressing pain points that impact their satisfaction and loyalty.

One of the biggest hurdles in creating a customer-centric approach is the existence of siloed applications and processes. Many banks operate with systems that do not communicate effectively, leading to fragmented experiences for customers. These silos create inefficiencies, frustrations, and ultimately the risk of losing customers to competitors who offer more cohesive and thoughtful solutions.

To build customer loyalty, banks must focus on improving the customer journey, whether digitally or in physical branches. It's about creating experiences that are not just functional but memorable. By breaking down silos, integrating processes, and designing every touchpoint with the customer in mind, banks can create a seamless experience that keeps customers coming back.

A truly customer-centric transformation is not just a strategy—it's a mindset. It requires teams to constantly ask: How does this benefit the customer? How does it solve their problem? How does it make their experience better? When we approach transformation with this perspective, we can deliver solutions that resonate deeply with customers and stand the test of time.

7.2. Evolving Customer Expectations

Customer expectations in banking have undergone a profound transformation over the years, driven by the relentless march of digitization. In the past, customers were content with traditional banking experiences—visiting branches, updating passbooks, standing in long queues to deposit money, or waiting for days for a funds transfer to complete. These delays and manual processes were simply accepted as the norm because there were no faster alternatives.

Imagine if a bank today insisted on maintaining such traditional practices. Would you choose to bank with them? The answer is a resounding "No." The modern customer no longer has the patience or willingness to endure inefficiency. Convenience, speed, and simplicity are now the baseline expectations, and anything less feels outdated and unacceptable.

Take, for example, the loan process. What once took weeks—gathering KYC documents, verifying income, and engaging in multiple face-to-face interactions—has now evolved into a 10-second journey for many unsecured loans. Today's customers expect immediate solutions, whether it's transferring money, applying for a loan, or opening an account. These shifts are not just conveniences; they are demands that banks must meet to remain competitive.

Looking ahead, the pace of change will only accelerate. Mobile apps and digital platforms are rapidly replacing physical branches as the primary touchpoints for banking. Soon, these digital channels may eliminate the need for traditional branches. As banks embrace tools like artificial intelligence, machine learning, and advanced analytics, customer interactions will become even more personalized, faster, and cost-effective. AI-powered chatbots and virtual assistants will handle complex queries, providing seamless service at a fraction of the cost and time.

To thrive in this environment, banks must continuously adapt. Embracing cutting-edge technologies, rethinking traditional processes, and anticipating customer needs will be critical. The expectation is clear: evolve or be left behind. The banks that succeed will be those that see change not as a challenge but as an opportunity to redefine how they serve their customers.

7.3. Enhancing Customer Journeys

To truly enhance customer journeys, banks and financial institutions must start with a deep understanding of their customers—their segments, categories, and unique preferences. In India, the diversity of customers is unparalleled, spanning different languages, literacy levels, and technological adoption. A "one-size-fits-all" digital strategy simply cannot address these varying needs. Having a world-class website or internet banking platform is impressive, but it won't serve every customer effectively unless tailored for inclusivity and accessibility.

For instance, the option to change the language on a banking app or website can make a world of difference, enabling customers to interact in the language they are most comfortable with. Simplicity is equally critical; transactions should be intuitive and effortless. Imagine the power of a voice-enabled application where customers, including the visually impaired, can navigate and complete their banking tasks seamlessly by speaking to the app. Such innovations are no longer a distant dream in the GenAI era—they are necessities that banks must prioritize.

One of the most significant aspects of customer experience is ensuring consistency across all channels. Omni-channel integration is no longer optional; it is the cornerstone of a seamless customer journey. While banks often offer various channels—websites, mobile apps, WhatsApp banking, and physical branches—they frequently operate in silos, leaving customers frustrated and disconnected.

Now picture this: a customer, let's call him Sudharshan, explores a car loan on a bank's website, filling out part of a lead form but dropping off midway. Later, when Sudharshan accesses the bank's mobile app or WhatsApp channel, he receives a friendly, personalized nudge: "Hi Mr. Sudharshan, we noticed your interest in a car loan on our website. How can we assist you further?" This kind of continuity not only makes Sudharshan feel valued but also simplifies his journey, allowing him to pick up where he left off on an entirely different channel.

This level of personalization and channel integration transforms a fragmented customer journey into a cohesive and satisfying experience. It shows the customer that their time and preferences matter, fostering trust and loyalty. Banks must invest in frameworks and technologies that enable this kind of connected experience—one where every touchpoint feels like part of the same conversation.

Enhancing customer journeys isn't just about adopting the latest tools or technologies. It's about empathy, understanding, and ensuring that every customer feels seen, supported, and empowered, no matter how they choose to interact with the bank.

In an earlier session, we briefly touched on the pivotal role of leadership and change management in driving digital transformation. This chapter dives deeper, highlighting the essential responsibilities of leaders on both the business and IT sides. It's not just about managing technology; it's about inspiring people, setting clear priorities, and fostering a culture that embraces change while staying laser-focused on delivering tangible business outcomes.

ROLES AND RESPONSIBILITIES: BUSINESS VS. IT LEADERSHIP

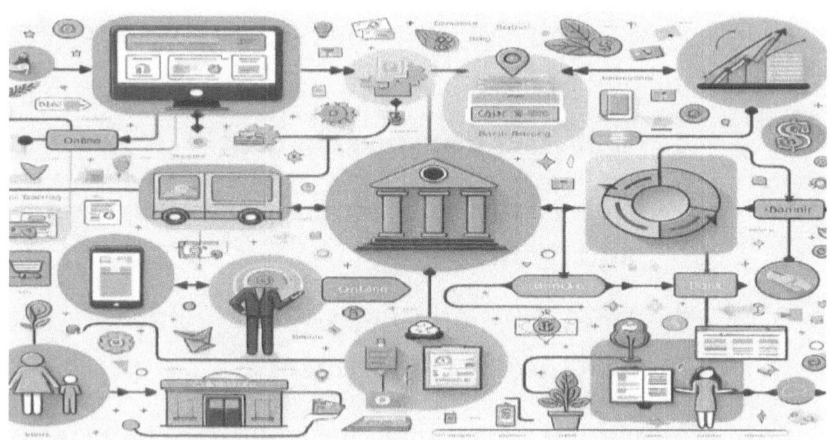

- **Business Leadership:**

  Business leaders are the visionaries of digital transformation. They must articulate a clear strategy, align teams to this shared vision, and focus on prioritizing initiatives that deliver measurable business value.

  - **Key Roles:**

    - Set and monitor processes for effective change management.

- Make decisions that prioritize critical and regulatory changes over "nice-to-have" additions.

- Ensure that every project aligns with strategic organizational goals.

- **Avoiding Project Dilution:** Too many low-impact changes can overwhelm teams and derail the quality of digital initiatives. Leaders should consistently evaluate requests based on three key questions:

  1. **What is the business benefit?**

  2. **How critical is the change in terms of effort and timing?**

  3. **Does the quantified benefit justify the cost and resource investment?**

- **Managing Resistance:** Resistance from business teams often stems from the perception that transformation efforts interfere with their "day jobs." Leaders must communicate that contributing to transformation is not just a short-term demand but a long-term investment in organizational success, benefiting individuals and teams alike.

- **IT Leadership:** IT leaders are the backbone of transformation, ensuring that projects are executed efficiently and aligned with the organization's goals. They must balance technical feasibility with business urgency, driving projects to completion without compromising on quality.

- ○ **Key Roles:**

  - ▪ Regularly track efforts, productivity, and progress.

  - ▪ Evaluate whether timelines for projects or changes are realistic and achievable.

  - ▪ Implement delivery in small, iterative sprints, achieving quick wins to build momentum.

  - ▪ Monitor the **Say-Do Ratio**, ensuring commitments are met consistently to build trust.

- ○ **Navigating Delays:** Delays can introduce complexity, as business processes may evolve during the project lifecycle. This can result in changes to original requirements, much like "changing the wheel of a car while driving at 80 km/h." Leaders must mitigate these risks by proactively managing timelines and dependencies, ensuring any changes are thoroughly evaluated for downstream impacts.

Driving Effective Change Management

Leaders are the custodians of change. Effective change management involves more than just tracking timelines or budgets—it's about fostering a culture where teams feel empowered and motivated to embrace transformation.

- **Steps to Foster a Digital-First Culture:**

  - **Educate Teams:** Help employees understand how digital initiatives contribute to long-term success, not just for the organization but for their roles and growth.

  - **Recognize Efforts:** Celebrate team contributions to transformation projects to foster a sense of ownership and pride.

  - **Encourage Collaboration:** Build cross-functional teams where business and IT work together, breaking down silos and fostering shared accountability.

- **Balancing Prioritization and Quality:** Leaders must be the gatekeepers of priorities, ensuring that unnecessary or low-impact changes don't dilute the focus on critical projects. A well-structured prioritization process allows organizations to stay agile while ensuring high-quality outcomes.

Building Resilience and Agility in Teams

- **Resilience:** Leaders must prepare their teams to adapt to unexpected challenges without losing sight of the end goal. Resilience is built through clear communication, structured workflows, and a commitment to continuous improvement.

- **Agility:** In today's fast-paced environment, agility is non-negotiable. IT leaders should adopt sprint-based delivery models, breaking large projects into smaller, manageable milestones. This approach ensures timely feedback, early problem identification, and consistent progress.

A Humanized Perspective

Digital transformation is as much about people as it is about technology. Business leaders must inspire and prioritize effectively, while IT leaders must deliver with precision and agility. Together, they act as the anchors of change, ensuring alignment, managing resistance, and driving success.

Leadership is not about being in charge; it's about taking care of those in your charge. By fostering a culture of collaboration, setting clear priorities, and building resilient, agile teams, leaders can ensure that digital transformation isn't just an initiative—it's a movement that propels the organization toward a future-ready state.

Reference from Thirukural.

On Collaboration and Unity

Kural 518

"துணையுடையான் துன்இல்லான் என்நோக்கத் திறனுடையான் துன்பம் வரின்."

Translation:
A man with dependable allies will stand unshaken even in adversity.

This highlights the importance of collaboration between business and IT teams during digital transformation. Unified efforts ensure resilience and success.

09

LEVERAGING DATA FOR TRANSFORMATION

In the era of digital transformation, data is more than just numbers and records; it is the lifeblood of a bank or financial institution. Data acts as both an input that powers decisions and strategies and as an output that reflects the effectiveness of digital applications. Yet, it is often observed that data doesn't receive the attention it truly deserves. This chapter emphasizes the importance of treating data as a strategic asset, harnessing its power, and ensuring its security.

Why Data is Critical for Transformation?

1. **Data as a Key Driver of Business Success:** Every bit of information—from customer profiles and transaction histories to behavioural patterns and operational logs—is a treasure trove waiting to be mined. Banks or NBFCs that invest in understanding, managing, and leveraging this data gain a significant competitive edge.

2. **Fostering Data Culture:** An institution that values data treats it as more than just a byproduct of operations. It becomes the foundation for decision-making, innovation, and enhanced customer experiences.

The Role of Data in Driving Decisions

- **Customer 360 View:** Imagine having a complete, consolidated view of each customer in one place—details about their accounts, loans, payment history, transactions, and behavioural insights all integrated. This is the holy grail of decision-making.

  - It empowers relationship managers with personalized insights.

  - It enhances credit decisioning with real-time data.

  - It improves cross-selling and up-selling opportunities based on customer needs.

- **Breaking Silos:** A significant challenge is the existence of multiple applications and systems within banks that don't communicate effectively with each other. This siloed structure prevents the consolidation of data into a central repository, such as a **Data Lake** or unified platform, limiting its utility.

- **Faster Decision-Making:** When data is readily available and well- structured, decisions that used to take weeks can now happen in minutes. The agility offered by a robust data framework allows financial institutions to stay ahead of the competition.

Data Security: A Non-Negotiable Priority

1. **Criticality of Data Security:** Data breaches or leaks can cause significant reputational and financial damage to an institution and compromise customer trust.

- o Protecting sensitive customer information (such as KYC, transactions, and credit data) is paramount.

- o IT teams must prioritize security measures like encryption, firewalls, and real-time monitoring to prevent unauthorized access.

2. **Regulatory Compliance:** The increasing focus of regulators on data privacy and governance makes it imperative for institutions to have robust data protection policies in place.

Harnessing Data for Innovation

1. **Business Intelligence (BI):** A strong BI unit acts as the nerve center for data analytics, providing actionable insights to management. This includes:

   - o Customer segmentation for targeted marketing.

   - o Predictive analytics for credit risk management.

   - o Real-time dashboards for compliance and audit reporting.

2. **Data-Driven Transformation:** By leveraging historical and real-time data, institutions can identify patterns, forecast trends, and develop innovative products that meet evolving customer expectations.

3. **AI and ML Integration:** Advanced tools like Artificial Intelligence (AI) and Machine Learning (ML) can further enhance the utility of data by automating insights and enabling predictive models.

Building a Strong Data Foundation

1. **Centralized Data Repositories:** Consolidate all customer and operational data into a unified Data Lake. This requires:

   - Proper data mapping and governance frameworks.

   - Regular updates to maintain accuracy and relevance.

2. **Data Governance and Ownership:** Assign dedicated teams or roles responsible for ensuring the quality, security, and availability of data across the organization.

3. **Investment in Technology:** Modernize legacy systems and adopt tools that enable seamless integration and analysis of data.

The Human Side of Data Transformation

For data to truly drive transformation, both business and IT teams must understand its value. Leaders must foster a culture where data is seen not just as a byproduct but as a powerful tool for growth.

- **Empowering Teams:** Provide training to ensure teams can interpret and act on data insights effectively.

- **Encouraging Collaboration:** Business and IT must work together to ensure data structures meet both operational and strategic needs.

- **Recognizing Data Champions:** Acknowledge and reward those who use data creatively to solve problems or drive results.

Data is the ultimate asset for any bank or financial institution. When managed and leveraged effectively, it drives faster decision-making, innovation, and improved customer experiences. However, with great power comes great responsibility—ensuring data security and privacy is non-negotiable. By investing in a robust data framework and fostering a culture of data-driven decision-making, institutions can unlock the true potential of digital transformation.

10

EMERGING TECHNOLOGIES AND THEIR ROLE IN BANKING

The pace of technological advancement is reshaping every industry, and banking is no exception. Banks and financial institutions are at a critical juncture where embracing emerging technologies is not just a competitive advantage but a survival imperative. In this chapter, we delve into the evolving landscape of technology and its transformative role in banking, discussing how institutions can harness these innovations to meet customer expectations, drive operational efficiency, and achieve sustainable growth.

The Technology Conundrum: Legacy vs. Evolution

One of the biggest challenges for banks is the coexistence of legacy systems and the need to adopt cutting-edge technologies. While legacy systems represent significant investments and often handle critical operations, they can hinder agility and innovation.

- **Core Stability, Edge Agility:** While the core banking systems may not require frequent upgrades, customer-facing applications, decision engines, and go-to-market platforms must evolve at the speed of industry innovation.

- **Balancing Investments:** Banks must strategically prioritize investments in technology, focusing on areas where rapid evolution can deliver maximum impact, such as customer touchpoints and real-time decision-making systems.

Key Emerging Technologies Shaping Banking

1. **Artificial Intelligence (AI) and Machine Learning (ML):**

   - **Predictive Analytics:** AI-powered analytics enable banks to anticipate customer needs, manage risks, and identify fraud with greater accuracy.

   - **Customer Support:** Intelligent chatbots and voice assistants provide instant, accurate support, enhancing customer satisfaction.

   - **Credit Scoring:** AI-driven models analyse vast datasets to assess creditworthiness more accurately and fairly, improving loan decisioning.

2. **Robotic Process Automation (RPA):**

   - Automates repetitive, rule-based tasks, such as account reconciliation and compliance checks, reducing turnaround time and errors.

   - Enhances operational efficiency and allows human resources to focus on high-value activities.

3. **Blockchain Technology:**

    o **Secure Transactions:** Offers a transparent and immutable ledger for secure, tamper-proof financial transactions.

    o **Smart Contracts:** Automates contract execution, reducing reliance on intermediaries and speeding up processes.

4. **Cloud Computing:**

    o **Scalability:** Enables banks to scale infrastructure and services based on demand.

    o **Cost Efficiency:** Reduces costs by eliminating the need for on-premises data s and enabling pay-as-you-go models.

5. **Internet of Things (IoT):**

    o Facilitates real-time monitoring of assets (e.g., in loan collateral management).

    o Enhances personalized customer interactions by integrating data from connected devices.

6. **Generative AI:**

    o Offers new possibilities in content creation for marketing, customer engagement, and personalized recommendations.

    o Can analyse unstructured data such as emails or voice interactions to generate actionable insights.

The Essence of Instant Decisioning

In today's world, speed is non-negotiable. Customers expect real-time services—whether it's opening an account, applying for a loan, or resolving a query. However, speed must not come at the cost of accuracy or risk management.

- **AI-Driven Decision Engines:** By integrating AI and ML, banks can process vast amounts of data in real-time to make smarter, faster decisions.

  - Example: Real-time credit scoring using AI models.

  - Benefit: Minimizes the risk of defaults while ensuring faster loan disbursal.

Balancing Speed and Analysis: Instant decisions should be backed by robust models that ensure both agility and accuracy to prevent losses.

Reference from Thirukural.

On Adapting to Change

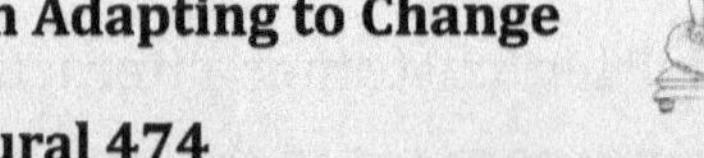

Kural 474

"யாமறிந்த மாந்தராய்க் காணின் அவரிடை நாம்மறிந்தது இல்லை எனின்."

Translation:
Acknowledge others' superior knowledge and adapt; accordingly, this is wisdom.

Adaptability is critical in embracing new technologies and methodologies. Transformation leaders must remain humble and open to learning.

Real-Life Applications and Success Stories

1. **Voice and Chat Bots:**

   o **Implementation:** A combination of voice and chatbots was introduced to handle inbound queries.

   o **Impact:**

      ▪ 60–65% of inbound calls were resolved by the voice bot, reducing dependence on call center agents.

      ▪ Freed up human agents to focus on high-value activities such as hard bucket collections and sales campaigns.

   o **Result:** Improved customer experience, enhanced productivity, and significant cost savings.

2. **Process Automation:**

   o **Use Case:** Automating 10 manual processes within operations, such as KYC verification and compliance checks.

   o **Outcomes:**

      ▪ 90% reduction in turnaround time (TAT).

      ▪ Zero error rate, eliminating losses due to manual errors.

      ▪ Significant productivity improvements, allowing employees to focus on more strategic tasks.

Embracing Technology with Purpose

The key to successfully leveraging emerging technologies lies in thoughtful adoption:

- **Identify Pain Points:** Begin with areas where technology can deliver the most value, such as customer service or back-office operations.

- **Pilot, Scale, Repeat:** Test technologies on a small scale before expanding their implementation across the organization.

- **Ensure Employee Buy-In:** Provide training and demonstrate how technology complements human efforts, rather than replacing them.

- **Focus on ROI:** Measure the impact of technology on business outcomes to ensure investments deliver tangible benefits.

Preparing for the Future

The next wave of innovation will bring even greater possibilities:

- AI will become more intuitive, enabling hyper-personalization of services.

- Blockchain will revolutionize cross-border payments and digital identity management.

- IoT and wearables will offer unprecedented insights into customer behaviour.

Banks that proactively embrace these changes and integrate them seamlessly into their operations will lead the way in redefining customer experiences and achieving operational excellence.

Emerging technologies are not just tools—they are enablers of transformation, agility, and growth. For banks, the challenge is not just to adopt these technologies but to do so in a way that aligns with their strategic goals and customer needs.

11

SCALING DIGITAL TRANSFORMATION INITIATIVES

Digital transformation often begins with pilot projects designed to test concepts, technologies, and strategies. However, the real challenge lies in scaling these initiatives to deliver value across the entire organization. This chapter explores the key considerations, challenges, and strategies for expanding digital transformation initiatives from isolated pilots to enterprise-wide implementations while maintaining momentum and avoiding fatigue.

From Pilot to Enterprise-Wide Implementation

Launching a successful pilot is only the beginning of the transformation journey. Scaling that success across the organization requires careful planning and execution.

1. **Evaluate Pilot Success:**

   - Assess the pilot based on predefined metrics such as ROI, customer satisfaction, efficiency gains, and employee feedback.

   - Identify elements that worked well and those that need refinement before scaling.

2. **Establish a Clear Roadmap:**

   o   Define a phased rollout plan, specifying timelines, milestones, and resource requirements.

   o   Include feedback loops at each phase to ensure alignment with objectives.

3. **Secure Stakeholder Buy-In:**

   o   Engage key stakeholders across business and IT functions to align on goals and expectations.

   o   Highlight the benefits demonstrated during the pilot to gain support for enterprise-wide implementation.

4. **Ensure Scalability:**

   o   Adapt the solution to accommodate the complexity of enterprise operations, ensuring it can handle increased workloads and diverse use cases.

   o   Test scalability in controlled environments before broader deployment.

5. **Maintain Focus on End Users:**

   o   Understand the needs of employees and customers who will interact with the solution.

   o   Provide adequate training and support to ensure adoption and usage.

Managing Complexity: Balancing Agility with Robust Governance

Scaling digital transformation initiatives often introduces complexities that can slow down progress or compromise quality. A balanced approach to agility and governance is essential to navigate these challenges.

1. **Define Clear Roles and Responsibilities:**

   - Establish accountability at all levels of the organization to avoid overlaps and ensure smooth execution.

   - Create cross-functional teams to address interdependencies between departments.

2. **Implement Robust Governance Frameworks:**

   - Set up governance structures to monitor progress, resolve issues, and ensure alignment with strategic goals.

   - Use dashboards and reporting tools to track key performance indicators (KPIs) and provide visibility to leadership.

3. **Embrace Agile Principles:**

   - Break down the implementation into smaller sprints or phases, delivering incremental value.

   - Encourage continuous feedback and iterative improvements to adapt to changing requirements.

4. **Leverage Technology for Simplification:**

   o Use automation tools to reduce manual efforts and minimize errors in scaling operations.

   o Employ advanced analytics to predict bottlenecks and optimize processes.

Avoiding Transformation Fatigue: Sustaining Momentum and Enthusiasm

Digital transformation is a marathon, not a sprint. Sustaining energy and enthusiasm throughout the journey is crucial to avoid "transformation fatigue" among employees and stakeholders.

1. **Communicate the Vision:**

   o Reiterate the purpose and benefits of the transformation at every stage to maintain alignment and motivation.

   o Use real-life success stories to demonstrate the impact of transformation on employees and customers.

2. **Celebrate Milestones:**

   o Acknowledge and reward the contributions of teams at key milestones to keep morale high.

   o Share achievements widely across the organization to build collective ownership.

3. **Focus on Employee Well-Being:**

   o Avoid overburdening employees with excessive demands during the transformation process.

   o Provide resources such as training, tools, and time to support them in adapting to new systems and processes.

4. **Foster a Culture of Resilience:**

   o Encourage a growth mindset, where challenges are viewed as opportunities for learning and innovation.

   o Equip leaders with the skills to inspire and guide their teams through uncertainty.

5. **Monitor Transformation Health:**

   o Regularly assess the organization's readiness, capacity, and engagement levels to identify signs of fatigue.

   o Adjust timelines and expectations as needed to maintain a sustainable pace.

Building for the Future

Scaling digital transformation is not just about replicating successful pilots—it's about embedding a culture of innovation, resilience, and adaptability into the fabric of the organization. By focusing on thoughtful planning, robust governance, and sustained engagement, banks and financial institutions can unlock the full potential of their transformation initiatives, delivering value to employees, customers, and stakeholders alike.

This approach ensures that scaling digital transformation is not only achievable but also impactful, creating a legacy of progress and innovation.

12

RISK MANAGEMENT IN DIGITAL TRANSFORMATION

Digital transformation, while bringing immense opportunities, also introduces complexities and risks that require careful management. In this session, we will delve into the critical aspects of identifying and addressing risks, ensuring cybersecurity, and meeting regulatory compliance requirements in the context of Indian banking and financial systems.

1. Identifying and Mitigating Risks: Addressing Potential Pitfalls

Transformation projects are inherently risky due to their scale and complexity. To navigate this successfully:

- **Strategic Risk Assessment:** Begin by identifying potential risks across technical, operational, and cultural dimensions. For example, legacy system failures or misalignment between business and IT goals.

- **Mitigation Strategies:**

  - **Set clear priorities:** Evaluate initiatives for business impact versus complexity.

  - **Pilot projects first:** Test new systems with small-scale implementations before scaling.

- o **Contingency Plans:** Prepare for failures with rollback strategies and defined response teams.

- **People Risk Management:** Resistance to change can derail projects. Continuous engagement, training, and clear communication are vital to align teams with transformation goals.

2. Cybersecurity in a Digital Landscape

As banks and financial institutions embrace digital transformation, cybersecurity becomes a cornerstone of trust and success. Key measures include:

- **Proactive Defense Systems:** Invest in AI-driven threat detection systems and establish a strong incident response protocol.

- **Zero Trust Architecture:** Move away from perimeter-based security to enforce verification at every access point.

- **Data Encryption and Tokenization:** Secure customer data during transactions and in storage.

- **Regular Audits and Penetration Testing:** Evaluate systems frequently to identify vulnerabilities.

- **Employee Awareness Programs:** Human error remains a significant risk. Conduct regular cybersecurity training sessions to reduce risks like phishing attacks.

3. Regulatory Compliance: Navigating Evolving Laws and Indian Standards

Banks and NBFCs in India operate under a complex regulatory landscape with stringent requirements from the Reserve Bank of India (RBI) and other governing bodies. Adherence is non-negotiable:

- **Know Your Customer (KYC) Regulations:** Ensure robust mechanisms for digital KYC, including video-based verification.

- **Data Localization:** Align with Indian laws like the Personal Data Protection Act (when finalized) to store and process sensitive data within the country.

- **AML and Fraud Prevention:** Leverage real-time transaction monitoring systems to comply with Anti-Money Laundering (AML) norms.

- **Audit and Reporting:** Digital transformation projects must build reporting capabilities for compliance officers to meet regulatory audit demands.

- **Keep Pace with Evolving Standards:** Periodically review and update processes to reflect new RBI guidelines or global best practices, ensuring the institution remains competitive and compliant.

Bridging the Gap Between Innovation and Risk

The goal of risk management in digital transformation is to create a balance where innovation thrives without compromising security or compliance. By embedding a culture of risk awareness, financial institutions can confidently embrace the digital age while safeguarding their customers and operations.

> *Reference from Thirukural.*
>
> **On Planning and Execution**
>
> 
>
> **Kural 467**
>
> "செய்க பொருளைச்சிறப்பொடு செய்யற்க செய்யற்க செய்தபின் செய்யாமை நன்று"
>
> **Translation:**
> **Perform a task with excellence; if it cannot be done well, it is better not to attempt it.**
>
> Adaptability is critical in embracing new technologies and methodologies. Transformation leaders must remain humble and open to learning.

13

BUILDING A SUSTAINABLE DIGITAL TRANSFORMATION STRATEGY

A successful digital transformation strategy isn't a one-time effort—it's a continuous journey that adapts and evolves with the organization's goals and the changing environment. To ensure sustainability, this strategy must emphasize ongoing improvement, long-term alignment with strategic goals, and robust governance to deliver consistent value.

1. Continuous Improvement: Adopting Kaizen Principles for Ongoing Refinement

The philosophy of **Kaizen**—a Japanese term for "continuous improvement"—is a cornerstone of sustainability in digital transformation. By adopting Kaizen principles, banks and financial institutions can achieve incremental but consistent progress.

Techniques for Continuous Improvement:

- **Feedback Loops:** Actively collect and analyse feedback from customers, employees, and stakeholders. Incorporate this feedback to refine digital processes, user interfaces, and customer journeys.

- **Data-Driven Decisions:** Use analytics to monitor the performance of digital tools and identify areas for enhancement. For instance, if a chatbot fails to resolve a significant number of queries, analyse the gaps and retrain it using AI and customer data.

- **Agile Framework:** Break projects into smaller sprints with frequent reviews and updates. Each sprint can incorporate lessons learned from the previous iteration.

- **Cross-Functional Collaboration:** Foster a culture of open communication and collaboration between IT, business, and operations to uncover improvement areas.

- **Celebrate Small Wins:** Acknowledge and reward incremental progress to keep teams motivated and aligned with the larger goals.

By embracing Kaizen, even minor adjustments can collectively result in substantial improvements over time.

Reference from Thirukural.

On Visionary Leadership

Kural 382

"தெளிவி லதனை தொடங்கார் இளிவென் பொறைசெய்யா தானுங் கெடும்"

Translation:
Those who act without clarity will find their efforts fail and bring them disgrace.

This aligns with the importance of clear planning and strategic vision in digital transformation. Leaders must understand and articulate the "why" and "how" of transformation before embarking on the journey

2. Long-Term Vision: Aligning Digital Initiatives with the Bank's Strategic Goals

A sustainable strategy must go beyond immediate results and align digital initiatives with the institution's broader vision and objectives.

Steps to Establish a Long-Term Vision:

1. **Define Clear Objectives:**

   o Identify what the bank aims to achieve in the next 5–10 years. For example, increasing digital customer onboarding by 80% or reducing operational costs by 50%.

   o Link digital transformation directly to these goals.

2. **Develop a Digital Roadmap:**

   o Break down the long-term vision into phases, each with specific milestones.

   o For example:

     ▪ **Phase 1:** Automation of routine tasks (1–2 years).

     ▪ **Phase 2:** Introduction of advanced analytics and AI-driven customer insights (2–4 years).

     ▪ **Phase 3:** Full integration of an omnichannel customer experience platform (4–6 years).

3. **Evaluate Strategic Alignment Regularly:**

   o Periodically assess whether ongoing projects are contributing to strategic goals. For instance, a new mobile banking app should directly improve customer acquisition or retention rates.

4. **Anticipate Future Trends:**

   o Incorporate emerging technologies like blockchain, quantum computing, or metaverse applications into the roadmap based on their potential to disrupt the industry.

Framework for Long-Term Vision Alignment:

- **SWOT Analysis:** Identify the organization's strengths, weaknesses, opportunities, and threats to ensure that digital transformation initiatives address critical areas.

- **Balanced Scorecard:** Use this tool to align transformation goals with financial, customer, internal process, and innovation metrics.

3. Governance and Accountability: Ensuring Consistent Delivery and Value Creation

Strong governance is essential to ensure that digital initiatives deliver value, stay on track, and remain aligned with the bank's goals.

Techniques to Strengthen Governance:

- **Establish a Digital Transformation Office (DTO):**

  - The DTO acts as the nerve center for planning, executing, and monitoring transformation initiatives.

  - Comprise members from business, IT, and operations to ensure a holistic perspective.

- **Define Clear Roles and Responsibilities:**

  - Assign ownership for each phase of the transformation. For instance:

    - Business leaders to prioritize initiatives and assess ROI.

    - IT leaders to ensure timely and efficient delivery.

    - Compliance officers to oversee regulatory adherence.

- **Implement Governance Models:**

  - Use frameworks like **COBIT (Control Objectives for Information and Related Technologies)** to manage IT governance.

  - Leverage **Prince2 or PMP methodologies** for project governance.

- **Monitor Progress with KPIs:**

  - Regularly track Key Performance Indicators (KPIs) such as:

- Customer satisfaction scores.

- Digital adoption rates.

- Cost savings achieved through automation.

- Time-to-market for new products or services.

- **Accountability Through Transparency:**

  - Conduct regular reviews with leadership teams to share progress updates.

  - Maintain transparency about challenges, delays, or deviations from the plan.

Building a Resilient Framework for Sustainability

To integrate all these aspects into a coherent strategy, banks and financial institutions can adopt the **Pyramid of Digital Sustainability** framework:

1. **Foundation (Core Systems and Infrastructure):**

   - Ensure the core banking systems and IT infrastructure are robust, scalable, and secure.

2. **Middle Layer (Integration and Data):**

   - Build seamless integrations between systems.

   - Create a centralized data repository to support decision-making and customer insights.

3. **Top Layer (Customer Experience and Innovation):**

   - Focus on enhancing the customer experience through innovative tools and platforms.

   - Continuously introduce customer-centric features.

4. Governance and Oversight (All Layers):

- Ensure every layer adheres to governance standards and aligns with the bank's strategic objectives.

A sustainable digital transformation strategy thrives on clarity, collaboration, and commitment. By embedding a culture of continuous improvement, aligning with long-term goals, and instituting rigorous governance, banks can navigate the complexities of transformation while delivering enduring value to customers and stakeholders.

Reference from Thirukural. 

On Accountability and Governance

Kural 514

"அறன்என்ப எல்லாப் பொருளும் திறன்என்ப தீமையும் அஞ்சு பவர்."

Translation:
Virtue encompasses all wealth, and only those who act with understanding avoid harm.

In digital transformation, governance ensures alignment with ethical practices and sustainable growth. Teams must act with integrity and foresight.

Case Studies:

Exploring global case studies in digital transformation offers valuable insights into the successes and challenges faced by banks worldwide. These examples highlight effective strategies, common pitfalls, and approaches to futureproofing in a rapidly evolving digital landscape.

Success Stories Across Geographies

1. **DBS Bank (Singapore):** DBS embarked on a comprehensive digital transformation to become "digital to the core." By integrating emerging technologies and fostering a startup culture within the organization, DBS enhanced customer experiences and operational efficiency. This approach led to DBS being recognized as the "World's Best Bank."

Knowledge@INSEAD

2. **Santander (Mexico):** In response to the growing demand for digital services, Santander launched Openbank, its digital platform, in Mexico. This initiative aimed to provide online banking solutions to the unbanked population and customers seeking better service, positioning Openbank as a significant player in the digital banking sector.

Reuters

Learning from Failures

1. **Digital Transformation Challenges:** A significant number of digital banking transformations fail

due to underestimating the project's scope and impact. Common missteps include lack of clear vision, inadequate change management, and insufficient alignment between business and IT. To avoid these pitfalls, banks should adopt a holistic approach, ensuring alignment across all divisions and incorporating emerging technologies and data throughout the organization.

<u>McKinsey & Company</u>

2. **Digital Disruptions in Nigeria:** Banks in Nigeria faced challenges during digital system upgrades, leading to issues like vanished funds and failed transactions. These disruptions highlight the importance of thorough testing and risk management during digital transformations to prevent customer dissatisfaction and financial losses.

<u>Business Day</u>

Future-Proofing Strategies

1. **ANZ Bank (Australia):** ANZ invested $2.5 billion in major technology projects, including ANZ Plus and Transactive Global, to counter competition and meet evolving customer expectations. This strategic move aims to reduce customer acquisition and service costs, enhance compliance, and improve cost-effectiveness, positioning ANZ for future success.

<u>The Australian</u>

2. **Digital Transformation Trends:** The banking industry is undergoing a major digital evolution, driven by economic unpredictability, the growing adoption of AI tools, increased emphasis on consumer privacy, and the widespread implementation of automated processes. Banks must prioritize smooth digital transformations to succeed in this shifting landscape.

<u>Finextra</u>

These case studies underscore the importance of strategic planning, customer-centric approaches, and adaptability in navigating the complexities of digital transformation in the banking sector.

Reference from Thirukural.

On Innovation and Growth

Kural 483

"அருமை உடைத்து உலகம் மருமை உடைத்து இல்லது உடைத்து.."

Translation:
This world belongs to those who overcome challenges and innovate.

Innovation is central to staying competitive in a rapidly evolving digital landscape. This reflects the core idea of leveraging emerging technologies and data for transformation.

RESEARCH AND REFERENCES

This book is built on a foundation of personal experience and publicly available research to provide a comprehensive guide to managing digital transformation in banking. While the insights and frameworks stem from hands-on expertise, extensive research from credible industry sources has been integrated to ensure relevance and accuracy. These references have been carefully selected from globally recognized organizations, research institutions, and real-world case studies to provide a well-rounded perspective.

REFERENCES

1. **McKinsey & Company**
   - Article: *The Future of Digital Banking*
   - URL: https://www.mckinsey.com

2. **Boston Consulting Group (BCG)**
   - Article: *BCG Digital Banking Insights*
   - URL: https://www.bcg.com

3. **Deloitte Insights**
   - Article: *The Future of Banking Ecosystems*
   - URL: https://www.deloitte.com

4. **Accenture**
   - Article: *Digital Banking Transformation*
   - URL: https://www.accenture.com

5. **PwC Global**
   - Article: *Banking and Capital Markets Insights*
   - URL: https://www.pwc.com

6. **Forrester Research**
   - Article: *Forrester Digital Experience in Banking*
   - URL: https://www.forrester.com

7. **World Economic Forum (WEF)**

    o   Article: *Shaping the Future of Financial Services*

    o   URL: https://www.weforum.org

8. **Harvard Business Review (HBR)**

    o   Article: *Aligning IT and Business Strategies for Transformation Success*

    o   URL: https://hbr.org

9. **Gartner Reports**

    o   Article: *Gartner Financial Services Insights*

    o   URL: https://www.gartner.com

10. **DBS Bank Case Study**

    o   Title: *DBS Bank's Digital Transformation Journey*

    o   URL: https://www.dbs.com

11. **Finextra**

    o   Title: *Digital Transformation in Banking: Get Rid of Illusory Expectations to Avoid Failure*

    o   URL: https://www.finextra.com

12. **Financial Times**

    o   Title: *What Are Banks Doing with Your Financial Data?*

    o   URL: https://www.ft.com

13. **FICO**

    o   Title: *Why Most Banks Fail at Digital Transformation and How to Avoid Those Pitfalls*

    o   URL: https://www.fico.com

14. **Cognizant**

    o   **Title:** *Case Study: Banking—How Digital Transformation Helped a Major Bank Get Closer to Customers*

    o   URL: *https://www.cognizant.com*

These references ensure a blend of strategic and technical insights, offering readers a robust foundation for navigating digital transformation.

These references have been instrumental in shaping the discussions within this book, providing real-world examples and reinforcing the strategies outlined.

I acknowledge the contribution of these sources in shaping certain sections of the book and thank the authors and institutions for making their knowledge accessible to the public. This declaration reflects my commitment to transparency and respect for intellectual property.

SUMMARY NOTE

This book reflects my experiences and insights, blended with publicly available research, aimed at demystifying digital transformation in the banking and financial services sector. In a world where technology is rapidly redefining how businesses operate; digital transformation is no longer optional—it is an imperative. But this transformation is as much about people, processes, and culture as it is about technology.

Throughout the chapters, I've strived to address the complexities and nuances of managing digital transformation. From identifying opportunities for change to building frameworks that ensure sustainable growth, this book walks through the intricate journey of reimagining banking processes for a digital age.

We explored the cultural and technical challenges that often hinder transformation efforts, emphasizing the importance of alignment between business and IT. I've shared real-world examples, practical templates, and proven techniques to help business leaders and IT teams navigate this journey together. Whether it's forming empowered transformation councils, evaluating vendors, or building a compelling business case, each chapter serves as a guide to foster collaboration and accountability at every step.

One of the central themes of this book is the shift in mindset—from viewing IT as a cost center to recognizing it as a profit enabler and a cornerstone of innovation. Digital transformation is not merely about implementing technology; it's about creating an ecosystem where technology empowers people, streamlines processes, and delivers measurable value.

I've also underscored the importance of fostering a culture that embraces change. Resistance—whether from business teams hesitant to adopt new processes or IT teams clinging to old ways—can derail even the most ambitious initiatives. By addressing these cultural challenges head-on and embedding accountability into the organizational fabric, we can pave the way for meaningful and sustainable transformation.

This book also highlights the critical role of leadership. Transformation isn't just a bottom-up or top-down effort—it requires leaders who can inspire, guide, and empower their teams to embrace change and innovation. A vision without execution is merely a dream, and leadership bridges that gap by setting the tone, aligning stakeholders, and driving the journey forward.

Ultimately, this book is not just about solutions or frameworks; it's about inspiring action. It's about equipping businesses with the tools and perspectives they need to thrive in a digital-first world. My hope is that the strategies and insights shared here will serve as a foundation for organizations embarking on their transformation journey and resonate with leaders and teams working to make a meaningful impact.

Digital transformation is not a destination—it's an ongoing journey of adaptation and growth. And while the road ahead may be challenging, it's also filled with opportunities to innovate, evolve, and deliver exceptional value. This book is my humble contribution to that journey, and I hope it inspires and guides you to create a future where technology and human ingenuity converge to redefine possibilities.

LIST OF ABBREVIATIONS USED IN THIS BOOK

Banking and Financial Terms

1. **NBFC – Non-Banking Financial Company** Financial institutions that provide banking services without meeting the legal definition of a bank.

2. **KYC – Know Your Customer** A process used by banks and financial institutions to verify the identity of customers.

3. **RTR – Repayment Track Record** A record of a customer's past repayment behaviour, used to assess creditworthiness.

4. **LAP – Loan Against Property** A secured loan where borrowers mortgage their property to raise funds.

5. **TAT – Turn-Around Time** The time taken to complete a process, often used in customer service and operations.

IT and Digital Transformation Terms

6. **IT – Information Technology** The use of technology for storing, retrieving, and processing information.

7. **AI – Artificial Intelligence** Simulation of human intelligence in machines that can perform tasks requiring human cognition.

8. **ML – Machine Learning** A subset of AI focused on creating algorithms that allow machines to learn and improve from data.

9. **BI – Business Intelligence** Technologies and practices for analysing business data to make informed decisions.

10. **CRM – Customer Relationship Management** Systems and practices that manage a company's interactions with customers and prospects.

11. **UI – User Interface** The point of interaction between the user and a digital device or application.

12. **UX – User Experience** The overall experience a user has when interacting with a product or service, particularly in terms of usability and satisfaction.

13. **API – Application Programming Interface** A set of tools and protocols for building and interacting with software applications.

14. **RPA – Robotic Process Automation** Technology that automates repetitive tasks using software robots or "bots."

15. **IoT – Internet of Things** A network of interconnected devices that can communicate and exchange data over the internet.

16. **QA – Quality Assurance** Processes and techniques to ensure a product or service meets defined standards of quality.

17. **C360 – Customer 360** A comprehensive view of a customer, integrating all data from various touchpoints and interactions.

18. **PoC – Proof of Concept** A demonstration to validate the feasibility of an idea or technology before full-scale implementation.

19. **SaaS – Software as a Service** A software distribution model where applications are hosted on the cloud and accessed via the internet.

Cybersecurity and Compliance Terms

20. **GDPR – General Data Protection Regulation** European Union regulation for data protection and privacy.

21. **ISO – International Organization or Standardization** A body that sets international standards, including those for IT and cybersecurity.

22. **ISMS – Information Security Management System** A framework for managing sensitive company information to remain secure.

23. **SOC – Security Operations Center** A centralized function within an organization employing people, processes, and technology to monitor and improve security posture.

24. **AML – Anti-Money Laundering** Laws and regulations aimed at preventing financial crimes like money laundering.

Digital Transformation and Change Management Terms

25. **BPM – Business Process Management** A methodology to optimize and improve business processes.

26. **ERP – Enterprise Resource Planning** Software that integrates core business processes like finance, HR, and supply chain.

27. **SDLC – Software Development Life Cycle** A framework defining the stages of software development, from planning to deployment.

28. **CI/CD – Continuous Integration/ ontinuous Deployment** Practices in software development to automate code integration and deployment.

29. **CX – Customer Experience** The perception and feelings a customer has about a company throughout their interaction journey.

30. **Kaizen – Continuous Improvement** (from Japanese) A business philosophy of constant, incremental improvements in processes.

A JOURNEY OF GRATITUDE AND SUPPORT

The road to success is never solitary, and I've been incredibly fortunate to have a circle of support that has shaped who I am today. As I look back on my career and personal life, I realize that it's not just my own effort but the guidance, love, and belief of those around me that has made all the difference.

At the very core of my journey is my elder brother, **Balaji**. He's been my role model, mentor, and navigator, ever since I can remember. As someone who is already established in the banking industry, Balaji's experiences and insights made it easier for me to chart my own course. His guidance was my compass, helping me through the darkest patches and blind spots that could have easily derailed my progress. I owe much of my career path to him. He taught me how to face challenges, and how to turn obstacles into opportunities.

I'm also blessed to have parents who gave me the foundation of love, values, and wisdom. I am proud to say I'm a "dad's child." My father's quiet strength, wisdom, and support have always been the bedrock of my life. They taught me the importance of perseverance, integrity, and always doing my best. Their constant encouragement gave me the confidence to go after my dreams, no matter how big or small.

Of course, my wife **Nishmaja** my better half, deserves a special mention. I'm lucky enough to have a wife who is not just understanding but also compassionate, someone who has stood by me through both good times and bad. Being a workaholic, I often find myself consumed by the demands of my career, spending less time with my family than I would like. Yet, without her unwavering support and patience, I wouldn't have been able to focus on my work with the same drive. She is the unsung hero behind every success I've had.

Beyond my family, I've been fortunate to have mentors and colleagues who believed in me and helped shape my career. **Mr. A.N. Raju** of Sundaram Finance, in particular, played a pivotal role early in my career. Though I worked with him for only a few years, the exposure and guidance I received from him accelerated my learning and growth. He taught me much more than technical skills—he taught me how to think critically, how to navigate the challenges of the corporate world, and how to maintain integrity in everything I do.

I also had the privilege of working with **Mr. Mohan Jayaram**, a person whose impact on my career is still felt today. I was fortunate to be part of his team in my early career days, and his influence remains with me. The fonts, colour themes, and language he introduced to me still shape my approach to work and communication. His attention to detail and his emphasis on excellence helped Mold me into the professional I am today.

There are two people I can never forget, **Mr. Sentamil Selvan** and **Mr. Alok Chadha** from Tata Motors Finance.

Selvan recognized my potential early on and took the step of entrusting me with opportunities that helped me grow in Tata. However, it was Alok who took me under his wing, challenging me in ways that were tough but rewarding. Alok was a tough boss, a taskmaster, but he brought out the best in me. People often remark that I am the one person who worked continuously with Alok for eight straight years, and that is a testament to the trust and rapport we built. His guidance helped shape my leadership skills and taught me the importance of discipline, focus, and pushing beyond one's limits.

I owe a special note of gratitude to **Mr. Arun Diaz**, who served as a board member in my previous organization. Throughout my journey, Arun Sir extended his unwavering support, guiding me both professionally and personally. His remarkable insights, coupled with his compassionate demeanour, left an indelible mark on me.

What stood out most about Arun Sir was his approachability. Despite his responsibilities at the board level, he was always willing to lend a listening ear whenever I sought his counsel. His ability to break down complex challenges into actionable solutions and his encouragement to approach obstacles with resilience have been invaluable lessons.

The trust and guidance he provided were instrumental in shaping my journey, and his belief in my abilities served as a source of immense motivation. To Arun Sir, I extend my deepest gratitude for his kindness, mentorship, and the invaluable wisdom he has imparted along the way.

These mentors, along with my family and friends, have all been crucial in shaping the person I am today. Success is never a solo journey, it's the product of the people who believe in you, who guide you, and who challenge you to be better. I am forever grateful to each of them. As I reflect on my journey, I can't help but feel an overwhelming sense of gratitude for the unwavering support I've received from my family, colleagues, and mentors. Their faith in me, even when I doubted myself, has been the driving force behind everything I've achieved. And for that, I will always be thankful.

www.ingramcontent.com/pod-product-compliance
Lightning Source LLC
Chambersburg PA
CBHW020543160726
47991CB00002B/563